tHe WriTinGs oF mE

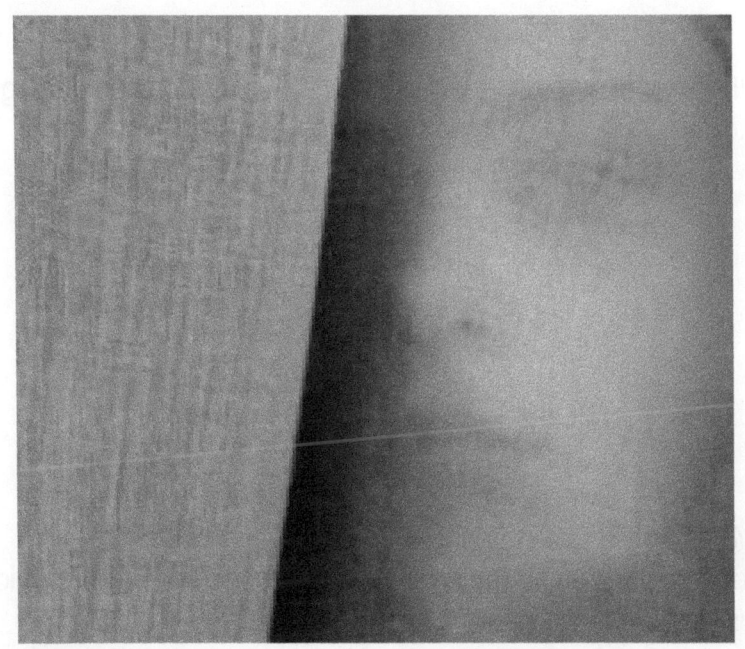

BrUised bUt NoT bRoKeN

Dedication
To those who endured my journey of joy, love, happiness, and pain......
To those that matter I love you all

"It is not the strongest of the species that survive, or the most intelligent but the one's most
responsive to change" ~Darwin~

Copyright @ 2011 Kenyata Fletcher.
All rights reserved, including the rights to reproduce this book or portions of thereof in any form.

ISBN 978-0-578-08068-0

Author: Kenyata Fletcher written between 1994-2010
Publisher: Kenyata Fletcher through Lulu.com

Printed in the United States of America

This book is composed of a variety of writings, poetry, and random entries. Representing my growth from a child to an adult, also written entries of experiences and emotions felt from some of those close to me. Outlining my journey of Love and Hate, my Pains and Endurance, it shows a true image of me, "Ms. Understood", in my struggles, my strength, my purpose, and my determination. Determination… not allow life to get the best of me for I AM A SURVIVOR of many things.
Journey with me

Warning: This book is composed of some detailed encounters and self exposure in detail. It **is not recommended for readers under fifteen** unless authorized by a parent. These writings explore love, sex, intimacy, nature, beauty, self-esteem, sexuality, abuse, and uncertainty. Please read with an open mind that a lesson was learned and a message is being sent.

Love Sick

Love has caught me by the hand; love has got me in a trance
When I lay down to rest feeling the sense of your head upon my breast
Hoping and wondering if you still feel the way I do
Only wanting you to never go through the things that I've been through
Ups and downs, ins and outs
wanting acceptance when I should appreciate me and you
Content with me loving you
but wanting and wishing to come back home
only to know we're all alone…
alone at last oh how I'm so glad
to see your smile and not a frown…
                                        to be continued

That special person

I would love to hold you in my arms and never let you go, but from my perceptions of what love is has not allowed me to grow. Comfortable enough to accept the challenge that it goes deeper than the thought, but still never wanting to loose you all at the same time. Confused with my actions versus my approach hoping to learn one day how to cope...cope and deal with that I must change otherwise I'll loose my love for being so vain. Through kissing you and touching you in the places that make you hot...arouses me. And from day to day only trying to keep you happy...happy that I'm here though very far...I must take the step and do my part. Because without you there is no me and without me there is no us for all eternity...

...Tell and show that special person you love otherwise good things can take a turn for the worse. And that good thing will be lost with only a remembrance.

A lost child

I am a lost child in this cold world alone left to find my way to better pastures over hills and ditches I climb only sometimes to feel left behind. Going in the right direction but not fast enough, is my past my future or is it all a dream. A dream that I want to awaken from and move about, a dream that I would like to let go. Something's in my present and past have kept me tangled, tangled from the outside world to see inside of me. Scars and bruises toils and tears have left remarkable impacts on me and it has caused me not to love some and not to believe…believe what people say deep down in my heart. It's a fight for all to get there and determination is the key yet being un-loyal and having limited respect is a set back.

Let one live to see the enjoyment that life has to bring…mistakes and challenges may come but even for those that are considered perfect it is still a step by step process and a lesson to learn by all…

A father's love

A father's love is only a dream for me. It exists but not to me because of my sexual orientation I have been disgraced. Disgraced and quoted that I will never succeed because that's not how God created me. Inside I hurt and long for the love that we once shared but it's gone for now and nothing compares. To my daily challenges of trying to be me and living my life happily all at the same time. When judgment comes that's my due date but until that happens I'll just wait and be me. And though my fathers love is near but far in my heart we are still apart. But by faith and the Grace of God we'll unite and be as one again until then **I LOVE YOU DADDY**.

A child's prayer

God gives me the serenity to be sane and just to look beyond the faults of others and into their hearts. Because we aren't perfect as people and we all thrive to get to what we need without even thinking. Our father above lifts our heads and our hearts…opens our minds so that we may see clearly…clearly that HE is the only way, truth, light, and if you follow him you will not be without. And for those that aren't it's a test of faith and a challenge to lift you higher. Trusts in the Lord for all things are possible through Him that loves us unconditionally.

Amen

Sweet Aromas

Kissing you gently from head to toe;
Kissing you up and down even in places that no one knows
Tasting and smelling scents pleasant to my mind
Wanting and longing to have you as mine
Mine again to taste again your cunt so pleasing to my tongue
The sounds you make when you cum
The aroma in the air
The aches and yearning that I feel even with more pleasure to spare
To see you aroused from the touch of my flesh with yours…
damn what a wonderful thing
We make waves and oceans as large as tubs
With the scent of your body and sex in the air
The movement of your ass and pussy so sweet
Is what makes a night of kissing you complete

Road Blocks

Just a remembrance or shall I say scar, a part of me has been taken away from my heart. The part that has left me confused at times. The part of me that is now left behind… Behind to fend on her own, as a seedling that has been planted alone. Alone in this big world with few by her side. Only for me to say hell it's not mine, not birthed from me but like my child. Sometimes we as people must part…part for the better and sometimes for worse but in due time it'll take its course. For the direction ahead is not yet given, just as life is not promised, but a brighter day is soon to come. So hold on to that remembrance or shall I say scar for it will be a guide along the way to help you with future situations that may cause you to stray…stay focused and **NEVER** give up!

Old Seems to Fade

Nothing meant to confuse you from my tongue, nothing meant to confuse your shaken heart. For I have all that I need…for He knows how much I can bear. Please be patient with me because I have no more spares…only "flats" that must go because they're no good only worn and weary.

Conversation empty but meaningful, clarity of confusing expressions
Exploration of my thoughts
Allowing you to get to know a piece of me
A side that goes unspoken
Not sure of the perceptions that may exist thus far
but realizing your eagerness to learn
You say look at the glass as half full
but how can I when I feel somewhat empty
Missing a link that may be valuable to my growth,
missing a link that may never exist, yet your patience is still like the night
for neither of us know what tomorrow may bring…
but fear will not keep us apart!
Until then you are in my thoughts and your situations are in my "Father's" hands

                                                        Sleep tight…

Random

Bickering bitches blab on about nothing. Selfishness and insecurities about life, but it's mine so what is your deal? Unexplainable attitudes that bounce high, emotions soaring, dramatic outside, and mentally unfit for the world. My life goes on though you would have wished it would end. You would have wished it would stop just like the aging process but that is impossible…no self-worth and no self-pity. Left behind like rust in a pipe yet you've blown and tossed me around tremendously. Well your time has come to be removed from my life so that you may spread your wings and begin to learn what life has to offer you…only without me.

Untitled

My expectations don't exceed too much.
My qualifications are just enough
Limitations to what I'm willing to experience
My heart open and hurting yet trying to maintain
The hopes of mending my pain…
Lost from reality…Hurt at home
Please sew my open wound
Protect me from evil, love me blindly, and keep me near
Help me mend my pain…
Although mild vibrations of anger exist
Pleasure overrides the sense of the unreal, the forbidden
My expectations don't exceed too much
My qualifications aren't enough
Because of the limitations that I'm not willing to experience
Yet I still have hopes to mend my pain

The Buzz

Gently admiring you from a short distance
Eyes tight and slanted high
The smirk on your face says more than your words
Your mind is wandering…off the potent potion that you intake
Intake to free your mind and relax your soul
You seduce yourself into your own world
The stroke of your arm and hand so soft
Makes your heartbeat and your lips sing
You sway back and forth in a desirable rock…
as if you are calming yourself from all your thoughts
You free your soul but it's impossible to relax your mind
You should have what you desire…

Foreshadowing images embrace my mind
The touch of your lips to mine
Images of bodies making graceful sounds
Your moans…the groans
Your insides warm and extremely moist
The sensations I feel to the sound of your voice
Extraordinary images with lasting impressions
Heart stopping moments without resuscitation
I open myself for you and you embrace the warmth
…we grow together

Obscenities flying undressed by emotions, revealed through temptations. Deceit lurking around the corner, Why question your fate or destiny? Open-handed options awaiting pick up. Disturbances occur, disruptions unnecessary. Ages brought to Life. True convictions hang high. Do you want this life that you have made for yourself or are you searching for peace or destined for Hell... You decide

Essence

Sugar sweet lips shine miles away
Soft brown skin like Oil of Olay
Almond shape eyes, full hips that smile,
short curls lay softly over your brows
Scented perfume lightly refreshing
Your smile so subtle but mysterious,
Loss thoughts compressed in the back of your mind
Expressions of joy lead you to a place out of the ordinary
Dreams full of sweet melodies that ring
Softly piercing each ear that I nibble at
Slowly licking you back and forth only to taste the
sweetness that your body has for me to explore…
Such a sweet delight

Show me

Share a moment with me like no other…
Teach me how to love
Teach me how to express myself
Show me how to have the energy that you possess

Share a moment with me like no other
Love me like I have never been loved
Take from me the things I know
Demonstrate for me…
Walk with me…
Be patient with me for I merely do not know…

…………how to show love that I feel

<u>It's been a while</u>

I yearned for you from miles away
We agreed to meet…from a few feet away
the blistering cold hardens your nipples…
(I am closer now)
Warm kisses moisten your forbiddens
The stroke of your neck and chest excites my emotions
Arousal hits its point and we begin to share sweat
Kissing viciously and grabbing you tightly
I pull you closer to feel my emotions
We interlock and your body softens
You melt in my arms and I catch all of you
We share a night like no other
We look into each others eyes and share one last kiss…
…….you sleep the entire night away

Stuck

I receive your response
It was enjoyable…
Passion burning and pinned up inside
Completing your satisfaction requirements
You accepted…
You desired, felt, and appreciated
Appreciated yourself for all of your accomplishments
Your strengths to move forward…
What a great push, a relief, a sigh of
imaginations soaring with possibilities
A future lies ahead…
It is incomplete yet semi-paved with bright yellow stones
a gold key to open the next door…
Will you accept your destiny or will you continue to lie
in the bed you just left

Lost without a path

How do you understand the mind of the confused?
How do you see through their flaws?
I get tense sensations and muscle spasms
My head aches and fingers twitch
My heart roars anger
My soul bleeds tears
Calming myself seems impossible,
Where does my future lie with all these built up frustrations?
How do I relax my innermost emotions and evident fears…?
Fears of hurting those close to me…
I ask the Lord to watch over me

Distorted Image

Unwanted taste of bitter images in my mind
Disturbing notions of your infidelity
Is the love genuinely real or just a part of your imagination?
Do you feel for yourself like you do for me?
Execution must occur to avoid all outcomes of disappointment
But how and why?
Is the decision to be made desirable real or faux?
Where do I place the sweet and sour taste that I hold near to me for you?
How do I blend it all together so that it is bold yet flavorful…?

Be free and honest with yourselves. Be goal orientated and self-directed. Look to the light and see the reality of life and what it has to offer. Accept your reality and follow your goals. Be mindful and prosperous with your decisions.

Thoughts of you are like a peaceful water streams
Sweet images of smiles like the sun
Your movements swift yet meaningful
Graceful curves move in the wind
Your heart like gold but soft enough for a push pin
You have purpose
You have life
Your desires have due dates
Emotions break dams and tears start flowing
Only to awaken to another glorious morning
You lie next to me but seem so withdrawn
Are your desires internal
Do they speak or are they silent like the night
Share them with me so that I can know your wants
Comfort yourself with my mild presence
Embrace yourself with my unforeseen laughter
Calmer than usual yet a blast
You have met one unlike any other
You have found internal peace
Your imagination runs wild with thoughts of all that you want to do, know, and share
Your growth emerges. You look into the tunnel and on the other end you see…you see me,
that comfort that has awaited your soul.

Betrayed

You call yourself a friend? How dare you use that term...
A friend is someone that doesn't feel the need to lie
Someone who can take constructive criticism and put it to use
Someone who desires to be loved without intimacy

So you think you qualify? How dare you...
You will lie and deceive me to have your way
You look to get ahead even if you have to misuse someone in the process of growth
I am only a convenience in your eyes

I say to you this is what I want in a friend...
A compassionate, understanding, embracing outgoing sister and friend
One who can warm my soul and console my inner emotions
One that has the same if not similar desires that I have and expectations of self
Can't be sometimey and they MUST be real

I thought that was you...but I guess we do not define FRIENDSHIP the same way!!!!!

I Enter You

I enter you…into your world, presence, and emotion
I enter your thoughts, imagination, and your images

I examine you
I examine your mind, actions, and your dreams

I comfort you
I comfort your spirits, desires, and needed touch

I inspire you
I inspire your goals, dreams, and your moves in life

I accept you
I accept your imperfections, human nature, and your ways

I receive you
I receive you into my life to share, grow, and learn

I desire you
I desire you to be the best at all you do and I am willing to support you along the way

Beauty

Your river flowed into my pool of open arms
You drowned at sea
Only to awaken to beautiful flowers and the musical underworld
You bloomed just as the flowers
As you opened yourself to me
You spoke the words I Love You
As I watched the words flow off your lips
Your breath heavy your heart free
Your eyes glisten in the dark
Your dreams of intimacy on a whole nother level excites me dearly
We explore what its like
The feelings of touch and beauty
The scent of fresh linen and roses
The strength that we possess
From embracing each other and stroking each others hand
……………………Nature has played its song

Random Thoughts

I write less than I use to. Is it because I'm less stressed or seemingly drama free? I'm not sure why it is that way, but my thoughts and my words don't seem to flow so properly. Clouded with future thoughts and plans…why not just deal with the present. I want to be some what prepared. I don't want to feel blinded and confused. Pray with me for I need a miracle too GOD…

Tragedy

Scattered brainwaves of contradicting thought
Emotions a lot less than before
Numb to the bullshit you seem to carry with you
Issues overbearing and burning so deeply
I feel the heat…
The heat that escapes my mind from the lies…
…hhhmmm (white) is what you'd call them
Manipulation had almost captured me
but my wall is great and built out of ancient stone
so its gonna take more than your bullshit and
manipulating ways to conquer that small crack you
thought you'd break…
you see for people like you, so sweet and innocent on the outside
yet thirsty and rotting inside
it takes a village to raise you but a dollar to break you…
see you deserve and desire the unseen future that lies ahead…
The dark road that you've so secretly paved
For your life is exactly what you have made it…
Your life is misinterpreted and directionless and in your mind
For that is what soothes you most
Loneliness is desirable for you…questionable misery is your thirst quencher
Love yourself my child for man cannot love you

On the Prowl

I lie in the shadows of a midnight forest
Like an animal lurking for its prey
I sit still and calm watching its every move
One wrong move and I will have nothing all over again
But nothing isn't so bad, when that something isn't as good as it appears to be…
See looks can be deceiving and I want the truth…
So I wait patiently for my prey to reveal its true face
It's true image of what the actual visage hides
the facade of life and all that it can offer

I sit watching like a thief in the night
for my prey to slip and let me in
Into their world to make a difference
A difference between the good and the bad
The evil and the unknown…
Is it worth my time…?
See I know what to expect from the evil but
…I am disturbed by the inconsistencies of the unknown
…I'll take the easy way out and deal with Evil

It is vitally important to know and find truth about yourself. God created you in perfection. You are God's masterpiece. You were created in the image of God. God loves you and wants you to be happy.

Moving too fast

Laughter from the unbelievable phrases that saturate my ear
Honest feeling is what you call it
Kids games is what it appears to be
Selfish gestures, inconsiderate actions. Why do you play games?
Where do you see a test?
I am only looking at you as you display yourself
But you think I'm wrong…
You think questionable thoughts because of my chosen pace with you
Do you even realize who you are?
Have you noticed your ways?
See I test you without even playing games
My watchful eye and observant ear examines you in and out
Your wants for maturity but lack of how to have it…
See you desire sympathy from many places only I'm not a stop
It is a syndrome that you have yet to shake…
The need to _HAVE_ abandonment issues
and the desire for those around you to sympathize for you…..

Life Long Labels

Small-minded   Imperfect   Close-minded   Maturity

Sweetheart   Complex   Intentions

Meaningful   Embarrassment

Insecure   Self-inflicted punishment   Pain   Doubtful

Loving   Extra Sensitive   Disappointment

Overbearing   Selfishness   Naïve   Emotional

Tease   Unsatisfied   Blunt

Soulful cries   Abandoned   Misused   Damaged

Inconsiderate   Bitch   Lesbian

Worthless   Misunderstood

Caring   Selfless   Wonderful   Beautiful

one in a million   Determined   Hard- working

Stupid   Spoiled   too critical on myself

……and thru it all, all I ever wanted was to be Free!!!!!

A new Beginning

Dark like a stain, but bright like a star in the midnight sky
A lonely road with eternal guidelines
Outlets that lead to something, who knows near or far
My only exit to free my mind of this blank sight of nothing
With only hopes of daylight but continuously missing it
From the blindness of wanting to Love and live in harmony…
Escaping the ties that bind me to this epiphany of…of an eternity
with internal and eternal desires to reach my light…
That light that can guide me to an abundance of joy everlasting
That light that makes my dark stain shine
Bright like no other…but now
My midnight sky is bright blue and peaceful as the oceans middle
My outlets have endings
Meanings, goals, wants, and promises
My outlets satisfy me
My blindness freed with all eyes open
I see a new place…a new beginning
and I am reaching for it…
…I have experienced my re-birth and I can't wait to explore its new meaning

Your 1st Time

A night like no other we grew
Connected internally by the attachment, but it goes deeper than that
Your passion both verbally and physically
You covered every angle
Satisfaction complete

Penetration long lasting and thorough
Your breath, you sweat, and moaned for more
Rapid gyrations that felt oh, so good
The stroke of the penis in everyway possible
You accepted me as a whole; you wanted more, the taste so desirable…
…you wanted more
We switch positions…and you wanted more…
Your voice still crying for more

A night like no other
Your passion both verbally and physically
You came (cum) over and over and over again
<u>We</u> covered every angle
and now your satisfaction is complete……
                      …a dedication to your first time

Is this a reality?

I saw you in my dream
Your touch and smell just as memorable as before
I liked what I saw, I envisioned our closeness
I felt your touch
Your juices overwhelming yet pleasant
Your conversation limited but meaningful
You expressed your love you're missing me
I was delighted to hear those words
I miss you 3x's much babe
The spirit behind our times spent
The memories that were good
Our downs not-enjoyable but the good in you rest above all else
You were my completion
Maybe spiritually you still exist
I'm unclear of all the above except the fact that I still Love you…
We connected exactly one month later how coincidental

Red Flags

What are the signs that teach you?
What are the signs that talk to you?
How do you read into them without getting hurt?
When do you decide enough is enough?
Do you love continuously… and can a burnt out fire be re-lit?
I love you means a lot to me
But my feelings mean more
Your skin, smile, and genuine character keep my heart near
Your swishy ways and double personality, demanding gestures, and high expectations
take my mind a far
I've wanted to love you fully in return
No added noise or strings still attached by others
but I feel like you deny me those rights
With tit for tat misunderstandings
How will we connect? How will we grow?
I'm getting older and you already know
where I'm coming from and how I'm tired of play
Unnecessary attitudes, people, and nagging personalities
Faux visages in the presence of others hurt me most…how can you hide unhappiness so well?
Is it because you are not unhappy, and would prefer for things to be like this?
There is a promised ending but never a guaranteed beginning…
Which would you prefer????

What's Truth?

If I allow you to love me
        Do you promise to have me until the end?
If I allow you to share my last breath
        Would you die for me?
To keep me in your arms as if I were your child
        To share my emotions we connect mentally
If you take me into one complete union
        I promise to make a way out of no way
To uplift our souls in puddles of tears
        We make love to happy hour
To share our thoughts and grow old together
        We become wise
If I allow you to love me
        Will you love me to the end?
                Love me through thick and thin…

Will you love me with your H.E.A.R.T?

My woman

The woman of my dreams will have a heart of gold
Her image pure
Eyes soft and brows high
A smile that travels continuously just as the street lights

The woman of my dreams must be strong with
endurance of a Tiger
Courage of a Lion
Yet sweet as a Lamb

This woman will have a spiritual connection and
Love herself dearly without being
Selfish but not too giving

This woman will be great
She will reign forever in my everlasting presence

This woman will be...
    She will be my...
        My Queen...
            My Woman

My Fear

My fear that is my time is coming close. My career lies ahead, but when will I reach it? Afraid of this day coming that will possibly be the kick off to the rest of my life. No emotions because of this boggled mind of mine. Right now I feel little. I almost feel slightly worthless with touches of a failure that is because so much of everything else is going on... Everything except the things that I need. Very few friends nearby that are on my level. How can I relate? Where and what do we have in common? How long will they stick around? Why do I detach myself from people around me? besides the need for space? I can't tolerate the amount of time expected. I don't fear my friends or my relationships but I do question the sincerity of the relationships. I think it's the fact that I don't want to waste my time on getting to know someone who is not sincere. I have friends that only rely on their issues and thoughts but what about my needs? Sometimes I require interventions but usually I resolve mine alone...I really need a break!!!!

Forgiveness

I forgive myself for not always having faith in me
I forgive myself for my selfish past, for allowing hurt and harm to remain in my life
I forgive myself for slacking when I was down and not doing my best
I forgive myself for not being honest and accepting of my sexuality long ago
I forgive myself for allowing others to get under my skin
I forgive myself for being imperfect and not having a way at this time, to understand that I was perfect in GOD's eyes and image

I love myself for believing that GOD can change all things and has total control of my life
I appreciate myself for having an open heart and mind despite my pain
I respect myself for remaining humble through rewards and losses
I treat myself to all that I need and not what I want
I love myself for always being honest with my heart and lastly
I love myself for being different from others…for being me

Love yourself in return

For what Reason

Don't try so hard to get noticed because you will go unseen
Don't work too hard at getting your envious ideas across because you will make a fool of yourself
Don't be spiteful and devious because you can, for it shows your immaturity
Don't be phony and shameful at once because it's contradicting

See I go unseen and heard like a thief in the night…
I speak truth and it hurts you, if you allow it, not me
I will not despise you for big or little things because I am able and willing to fix those undesirables from within myself
I will not be phony and regret it later for I will stop being your friend

So many people worry about the dumbest shit…well here is my reality check. Check your self issues and worry about you before looking my way!!!

Common Ground

Where is my common ground between love and pain?
My emotional instabilities and lack there of to feel…
I lack love and the ability to receive it, or that is what is perceived from those around me
But why can't it just be…
Be the way that I love, the only way I know how
My dreams of happiness and one partner complete
Will it ever come true or continue to remain…
remain the dream that plays over and over again…
Where do I go wrong? Can I feel like you?
How can this "cold" heart feel a warm breeze?
How do I connect?
For I have a lot to give

Emotional Peace

My facade is as tough as leather skin
My baggage light and limited
My thoughts heavy, my love strong
I've felt before but like a hot plate the touch became undesirable
Open to change…although bias run parallel to my emotions
Where is my turbulence for all…I want to feel more

My facade is as tough as leather skin
My baggage light and limited
My heart is of soft stone…like a mineral that dissolves over time
My trust factor is like my ex factor no definite obligations
So what do I hold on to?
The love that I have for myself to know that I am stronger than any emotion unclear…
The clouded images speak to me
The shapes, the movement becomes clearer but what is it that I see…

My facade is as tough as leather skin
My baggage light and limited
My thoughts heavy, my love strong
I just want to free my mind to set my soul free
To experience expression, life, and love entirely

To breathe in positivity with every breath earned

To enlighten others with what I have learned
To be free as a bird
To soar at any given time
To not have so many limitations that reduces me to be…
to be exactly what I am today an unstable, unemotional, human beast that's looking for emotional peace

Valuable Lessons

Valuable lessons are learned in time. It's the difference between love and hate. It's the moment that adds another minute on to time. Valuable lessons show you the meaning of life and friendship. Trust and honesty, Will you lie to me? Will you break my heart? Do you know how important it is for me to understand a lot about you so that I can protect myself from your finicky ways? See I value my feelings and reasoning above all else. Your purpose in defining my self worth and the diminishing of my character to others may not define the aspects of love that you have for me. You despise my thoughts to the point where you will justify every logic of meaning and non sense that escapes your tongue. But what about your flaws? Do you really think I should begin counting? Judge only your actions and words for you share as much wisdom as I do. Listen to others sometimes and not just yourself!!!!

Continued Resistance

Desperate for communication
Wanting to fix what's broken
Mending the few tears of existence
How do I connect to you?
Is it that your desire of loving me isn't worth the understanding of why am I so unclear
You seem to read between the lines any other time
This plan to avoid the same mistakes over and over again is incomplete...
Incomplete with answer yet no acceptance
Reassurance not guaranteed but granted...
Granted that I have all the strength and will to involve us in a plan
To recall my world of loneliness as a joint fixture that operates as two
Desperate for communication wanting to fix what's broken
Mending the few tears of existence
How do I connect to you?

Untitled

Days long and evenings diminished
Nights limited to nothing
No circle to free myself of daily emotions
No inner being
Dead silence in empty corridors
Longing for a shared breath or wind
Friends and foes limited to none
Life full of great opportunities
But short in passing
When will my time come…?
You see, I love hard and selectively
My happiness is deep
So deep inside that I have trouble understanding it myself
I want to feel and see normally as others do…
But not through the eyes of a self proclaiming "know-it-all"
For in a world like that I'll never get ahead
I want to feel and see as normally as others do…
With the realization that I am human too
My thoughts, interpretations, comprehensions, and actions may not be as such
but understand I am not you
I can love you or leave you, but you would rather understand me

Acceptance

I come to you with open arms but you are locked
Intertwined in a web I'm awaiting for you to surface so that I may rescue you from the difficulties you have with freeing yourself
The underlying surface of the situation just as shallow as an empty heart
We connected just at the wrong time
Your innermost feeling of isolation and frustration that your last experienced caused you
Overburdens your trust toward life and others
Emotionless to the desire for intimacy or another partner
The lies of the mouth and the betrayal of the heart has scarred you
I open my eyes to you so that you may see and explore new things
I open my hands to you so that I may lift you to a higher ground
But most importantly I open my heart to you…
…To share an eternal love with you

A passing moment of you……

Your lips shine and your hair flows beautifully in the wind. The soft touch of your hand strokes my cheek. The embrace from your hug secures my sense of intimacy. The music I hear when the wind blows, the feelings I catch upon your scent… I am imagining love. The type of love that will carry us through and through.

My hands felt you. You were soft as a baby's bottom, breast beautiful, eyes smiling and dancing in the night. A vivid image emerges and you were just as shapely as before. Intellectual abilities run miles long. Cultivating wonders travels that sparkle my soul. You are unthinkable, unbelievable like a magical moment.

She is Her as Her is me

She reports feelings of embarrassment and shame
She feels abandoned, alone, and rejected by even those that don't matter
She explores her opportunities but like an annulment it leads to a dead end

She reports being tired and confused but unwilling to give up HOPE just yet
Held captive by her thoughts of determination she suppresses her emotions and desires for change
...Her emotions which reflects happiness, and joy without pain

She enhances her spiritual desires to be guided through the right paths of LIFE
She tightens her circle and pulls on her reigns shortening the time frame of her dismay

She steps out on faith...as she reports her readiness she is no longer blinded
Although obstacles remain temporarily she follows her heart...
Which leads her to a field of harmony and bliss

She never looks back…

Untitled

Individual choices kept us apart. Desires to make alterations to who I was. Feelings of being inadmissible to your standards. Now you say you miss me…you think about me all the time. Your current relationship insufficient to what you thought you desired. Now you are… You are damaged internally because you let me go and I'm supposed to have a heart. My feelings are at a bare minimum.

So many times people communicate their desires to see something different as if my heart isn't enough. When do people see beyond the surface level facade and begin to digest…the realness and criteria that I possess. I prefer a worthy, ambitious, unpretentious kind of person to complete me. See relationships and true unions are what we make them. All our desires should not come with ultimatums sometimes we must look beyond our demands.

So ask yourself, "Who have you tried to alter?"

Life

As the tables turn, the mind begins to wander… Imagining all of what it could have been. Life's mishaps prevented you from looking further beyond. Beyond, into what could be a start of a good life. A life that could flourish from smiling, dancing, and laughter. The times that we enjoyed! Abandoning "love" from my rejection of the persistency. See I believe in natural occurrences that prove meant to be…not forced ones full of broken promises and promiscuous journeys.

From the moment I met you, you were destined to be known. Your energy, your spunk…although sometimes a bit over the top…it connected people. Your personality created by what you thought people desired you to be. What ever happened to being who you are? Picture perfect in theory but beyond that just an un-lucid reality. Obligated in your eyes to be all that you could even if it means sacrificing your identity. Indulging into a lifestyle not of your kind. You captured each moment as a lasting image, a permanent impression whose original template was altered. You became tailored made to my wishes. But the person that impresses me most is one who doesn't work so hard to be noticed.
Like a wind storm stuck in motion you brought the full effects of the earth in with you. With each day you pushed, pulled, the consistency hardened my spirit. Turmoil, rage, many broken pieces in the air…everything that one doesn't enjoy!

A labyrinth with no ends no exits. I believe in gentle kisses and accidental brushes of your hand against mine… I think about the innocence we once had and the moments we indulged in passion. Sometimes I can still smell you on my skin. The sweetest fruit bruised by forceful picking, let it ripen with the sun. Now it's bitter not ready to rest against the pallet. How exquisite to see beauty blossom before you. Fading into nonexistence Shadows of what could have been…Fade into the past!

Loving Hard

Loving hard is not always bad, not knowing when to put aside that love is more dangerous.
I have loved you for many years and I always will because it was something special for me. I could never forget the way you cared for, protected me, and loved me, among many other things. I know things were not always perfect or right…they were difficult and sometimes very frustrating but I was by you through thick and thin. Our love was tested and the struggle to maintain it was even harder. Our common link Enrique, feelings of abandonment and pain…I only know that I am always going to be here for you and you never have to worry about being alone. Trust in GOD and keep praying for strength because I will love you and him throughout my days.

For You and Him

Adorar Duramente

Para adorar duramente no es siempre malo, no sabiendo cuando a abandonó ese amor es más peligroso. Te quiero durante muchos años y yo siempre hago porque fue algo especial para mí. Yo nunca podría olvidarme la manera que usted cuidó de, me protegió, y me adoró, entre muchas otras cosas. Sé que cosas no fueron siempre perfectas ni correctas…fueron difíciles y a veces frustrando muy pero estuve por usted por grueso y delgado. Nuestro amor fue probado y la lucha para mantener que fue aún más duro. Nuestro lazo común Enrique, los sentimientos del abandono y del dolor…yo sólo sé que yo siempre estaré aquí para usted y para usted nunca tiene que preocuparse por ser solo. Confíe en DIOS y mantenga orar para la fuerza porque te quiero y él a través de mis días.

Para Usted y para El

There were many days that my heart was heavy and burdened with pain. I wanted nothing more but an out to escape my misery. On this one particular day I was in tears sitting on my bathroom floor questioning my purpose and wondering why was I put here to experience so much pain. Thinking of how I could end it all…would pills do it? No, because I didn't have anything. I could always cut my wrist…but I tried that before and I was told I did it wrong. I thought for a moment and figured well maybe I can get it right this time. I decided to break a picture frame and slice my wrist again… (Missing my main vein ¼ inch per the doctor's report I have failed again). I started to get pissed because I seemingly couldn't do anything right. So at that point I decided to call on the name of Jesus. I kept crying and crying, *"Oh Lord help me, and if you say you will be here in my time of need Oh God I desperately need you. You said if I have faith you will keep me"* still very tearful and contemplative my doorbell rang and interrupted my thoughts… Confirmation that GOD is always watching and ready to intervene in OUR plans!!!!

Listen to the plan that HE has laid out for you. I now can say I have so much more to live for and my story may help someone else who is ready to give up.

Untitled

Inspiration and imagination wander lonely in the night. Awakened to the early morning dew. Misting showers of glory moisten my skin. Sunflower petals caress my steps…I'm waiting…I'm waiting for my cloud from heaven is to come for me. To show me some royal entertainment and energy. To remind me of my destiny. To release my inner peace and make me bold and beautiful. To give me the road map that shows my future…my future paved of a golden road lies ahead. It's my riches, my destiny to place me in a comfortable and rewarding life ahead.

Choices

As I continue to open myself up for change I become uncertain as to the purpose. I feel that some people are one sided in their viewings and unintentionally selfish in their ways.

Life is a journey that we all must overcome eventually or "IT" will be the destruction of our intended paths. Decisions can destroy us or build us and making strategic moves can become more important.

In my journey I've chosen to do the best that I can without altering who I am as a person. I made both good and bad choices but in the end I have learned from my past…my mistakes…my continuous obstacles and I climb each hurdle with my head up high.

I refuse to hold myself hostage of my past!!!

<u>Freedom</u>

My daydreams turn into nightmares and my nightmares have turned into a reality. A reality that can't be frayed or revised. My delusions a midst over a never ending ocean. Vivid wonders of imagination come true. Questioning of all the things I can do…to explore my thoughts and awaken my mind. My spirit speaks to me silently telling me to let go and let give. Of all the heartache and misery you have put me through. Of all the inconsistencies and minor conceptions that are fictitious and null. To let go and rediscover my new beginning the beginning of a new me. The beginning of my Happiness and the end of this illusion of Misery!!!

A stressful year with extended weeks. A weekend so pleasant and needed it's complete. The thought eases my pressures, a clear mind, sounds of nature, and the smell of manure. All the necessities to the beginning of creation. Firewood burning while dark is nearing, silence drifts over the sky. Night falls near like stars that touch the ground. Can heaven get any closer??

My guards down and my heart lukewarm I feel loved…loved genuinely and unconditionally. So pleasantly enjoyable can this be everlasting or a figment of my imagination…There is a first time for everything. Yet so imperfect, I am still desired and craved. My scent is enough to trigger the Fourth of July in the middle of winter. Why me?? A stressful year with extended weeks. A weekend so pleasant and needed it's complete…Can this be?? Is it real or just a figment of my imagination waiting to fail??

P.I.T.Y. (putting in too many years)

I bled for you,
I cried for you
I ached for you,
I mourned for you...yet
You never acknowledged the good in my existence, you were never satisfied
An old wise tale said misery loves company. Why didn't I see the signs?

I sacrificed for you,
I praised your intelligence
I was appalled by your ignorance
I was shattered by confrontation...but
I loved you throughout even when there was no end
I desired you to reach your senses but with all things it was too late

I accepted your change,
I stood up for our beliefs,
I challenged you mentally...yet
You manipulated every word that came out of my mouth
You thought of me as a child without thought
You desired complete submission...how one-sided were you?

You changed me
You made me sad, angry, resentful, jealous, envious, and ashamed all at the same time. You caused many mixed emotions, you made me hate myself more and more
I hated you but I also loved you as God's child
I wished karma upon you so that you may develop a new heart
I wanted you to learn the difference between control and love...

...but first I had to learn that I was the only one doing, trying, and giving

I had to learn that I had nothing else but me…and for you that would never be enough

So once I left…

I didn't cry for you,
I didn't yearn for you,
I didn't mourn for you,
I didn't hate you
I didn't knock you for your own personal blockage and failures
I didn't allow you to have the best of my emotions anymore
I loved myself
I nurtured me, and I praised myself for finally taking care of me

Lost time drifted away!! If you do nothing else in life always love yourself 1st and never allow anyone to change that!

Tricks of Trade

Crossing paths with one from the past. How interesting can the conversations be? Interrupted by all the thoughts of deception that took place in your moment.

Should I be cruel or should my conversations be pleasant knowing the lies that surfaced with out interaction. Nice and Lovely is how the image is presented. You are a masked devil without its horns.

Nothing but an associate with a distorted point of view. No ulterior motives or intentions beyond friendly convo. But when your purpose is to be noticed, heard, and remembered I guess you would have nothing but exceptional conversation for most!!!

A trick turned suburbanite....no different from a hoe turned into a house wife. Wow what relocation can do to an individual... it can give you powers beyond belief that even you will attempt to remove your past.

Well little Ms. Uppity reject, your hoe card was pulled and I'm one bitch that never made your team.

My pen the speaker of my emotions
My thoughts a bitter sweet notion
To live or die is a neutral feeling
Rejection, denial, and only my sense of self worth
Anger from my need to succeed
Frustration from the trials of failure
With my pen the speaker of my emotions
Can I be the center of my misery?
I want to feel as you do
I desire to be loved accordingly
Shame free with no traces of bitter sweet
Only enjoyable thoughts and…
My mouth to be the speaker of my emotions

So uncertain about the things I have to offer. Felt complete about my start to a positive change. Unsure about so many things about me. Yet some disagree about the things that I see. Not sure of why I lack the ability to show my interest. Which sucks because it throws me off. I'm not too far from it, but where does it lie? How can I loose the interest of what could be the only thing that I see fit right now?

Confusion

Fear that leads me into darkness
Like an addict in rehab
Frustrating moments and the inability to practice patience
Wanting the urge to go away
My craving for you sits deep in my heart
Like a drug in my mind...
You fucked up all my mental
Like a thief in the night you robbed my heart
I needed you but you left me lonely
I searched for you but you were gone without notice
Your heart sings songs to me that carry like dander in the air
Bellows of will you marry me not later but soon...
I'm connected to you by feeling and heart
My soul won't let you go but my mind mourns with weakness
Fear that lead me into darkness
Like an addict in rehab
I no longer desire you...
I don't need you although my heart bleeds you
Let me heal
Lord walk with me through this journey
Provide the light by letting me give breath to another
Let me love continuously without pain
Allow me to loose you in my memories
But keep you locked away in my heart
It's the fear that lead me into the darkness Like an addict in rehab...but none the less with a successful recovery.
(Confusion cont'd)

My fears can no longer blind me they cannot hold me back I must grow as a caterpillar did into a beautiful butterfly. I will not surrender myself for misery.

Center of reality
Envisions of power
Power to love, connect, and to be free
Illusions of helplessness
With strength as my chaser
I have drank my misery
Courage of all men stand strong
Wisdom to maintain
Peace to get through
Values to hold on to and create that better person…
A person that is endeavored
That person is…
my…
…….my self esteem

I have let go…I have defied my heart
and the only thing that I have loved more than myself
My heart aches but my inner soul feels relieved
My time will come
Definition will be laid out
And a detail explanation will be given
The churn in my stomach gives acid reflux in my throat
I am sickened to the point of no turning back.

Memories never forgotten

Friends define the meaning of a thin line between love and hate. A lesson learned that can change the heart. A mindful experience that can cause turmoil. An evening of pleasure can turn into a night of horror. Questions gone wrong. Communication confusing and limited. Untangle this web of confusion, commitment to self and her, challenging situations, and heart broken memories. I hurt, I cry, I bleed. Bruises leave broken scars and fractured veins cutting off my circulation to life, to others, to destiny. Can I share? will I feel? is it time? Opening up my heart is sharing my wisdom and all that I have. My life is private and personal. My best kept secret and getting to know you must be special. You must be defined as belief, as life, as a token appreciated. As a friendship felt and never ending.

New York 2001 Twin Tower Disaster

We remember the survivors and the deceased
The regrets of never sending our last...I love you
The families that ache continuously with no medication
Such a terminal disaster
Lives ruined yet a positive ending
God holds them dearly in a special place
He keeps them as his gatekeepers with watchful eyes
protecting all others with their special signs
The signs that everyday Americans miss out on
R.I.P. to all the deceased, their survivors, and their children

Y.A.O.A..U.J

Embracing the enjoyment of continuous growth
Learning about self and self needs
The circle of life incomplete because I don't have you
My fears closed within and the mental destruction that I am experiencing overflows
Like roads gone unfinished and my heart only half-way broken
hanging on only by a vein
Life is such a powerful lesson
It stands out like Jesus in Galilee…a Jew
It has strength yet can be broken into pieces to prove its point.
To remind us never to walk around with our eyes closed
A remembrance of sacrifices and obstacles conquered
Embracing the enjoyment of continuous growth
Learning about self and self needs
The circle of life incomplete
Where will my soul lie? Will my heart remain broken?
Well only time will tell and love will heal
My life long lesson begins from within
My daily fears will be overcome in time…
and in the end through all my lessons, love, and pain
The question still remains
Will I have you? Do we have purpose?

The Chase

Energy lifted by the magnitude of the clouds filling

Restful vineyards produce bold flavors of delight

My wants, demands, and expectation of character

So perfect and flavorful

My nose inhales compassion and my soul exhales relief

Constipation once caused by agitation suddenly swept under the door

The world, connection of self, and potential to soar

I'm determined, I fly high, and I soar with

Energy lifted by the magnitude of clouds filling

Restful vineyards produce bold flavors of delight

I taste sweet perfection and want only the best

Drowning

Days, weeks, and nights of loneliness unforgotten
Difficulties passing by
Emptiness unchanging, bold reflections of memories, joy, and life
Concerns of my to-comes
Sacred securities unrevealed
Insecurities printed boldly across the sky
Happiness walks in and then by
A foot away from a saving raft
I missed it, again I slipped,
My first love innocent and pure like music to my ears
Harmonious tunes enlighten the memory
Angels above keep me grounded for there is HOPE, DESIRE, and LOVE
Just as innocent and peaceful as the first time I embraced it

The Run around

Tired, exhausted, and relieved
Set free from a misery that I may have been preparing for myself
Her gentle approaches comforting
Your reality is that I am unprepared for I have yet to mend…

Tired, exhausted, and relieved
My soul set free yet my mind bleeds…
Bleeds confusion and disbelief of the happenings to me
I am unclear of the whys, but sure of the why nots
For you don't bring out the best in me

So I am tired, exhausted but now relieved

My physical emotions challenged and censored
Packed away like the secrets of Pandora's Box
Filtered away from all connections

My physical emotions disconnected but have yet to disappear
With slight existence only for special hearts
You see I can't feel for everyone and everything
I can only be me

My physical emotions challenged and censored
Packed away like the secrets of Pandora's Box
Filtered away from all connections
I want to be free…
Free with my physical emotions
Open for intimacy of the mind

To have a connection with a perfect fit
I desire it but my mind and body are working against me

Desolation

Dark skies with hidden lights encompass the earth and prevent twinkles...
Equivalent to an empty bed occupied physically but without hope
Hope that tomorrow may be slightly different than the previous day
Hope that somewhere behind the dark skies filled with hollow clouds exist light

A representation of what is missing from ones heart as emptiness exist alone
The idea that somewhere deep inside lies a person awaiting to have life...
Life in abundance, life that reflects joy, the life that was planned for them

They say at the end of every rainbow lies a pot of gold
A heaven awaited with angels flying high
A serene garden with scents of orchids and water flowing gracefully through a stream
The dark skies have lifted, hope is being instilled, I live life and I experience being fulfilled

My 1st Love

I knew this man from afar yet I rested my heart and soul in his spirit
Though wishy washy I trusted him to protect me
This is the man who betrayed my trust and love for nothing
Though young and naïve to the word LOVE I loved him, and I loved HARD

He was my world, my all from the sunlight to the moonlit path
He was the tick of my clock
His caring and insensitive ways confused my inner emotions and I doubtfully questioned his concern for me
Though young and naïve to the word LOVE I loved him, and I loved HARD

The man who catered to my illnesses and stroked me gently to sleep
He ignited fires that winds couldn't sweep
Both good and bad, happiness and anger got the best of me
My emotions shaken and shattered all at the same time
But I loved this man and I loved him hard

He kept me close like he owned me only to push me away with hate
But why I never shamed him or faulted him for any of my unforeseen depressions or doubts of bitterness

This is a man that I worshipped like none other
this was my man...

The man who betrayed my trust and love for nothing though young and naïve to the word LOVE, I loved him HARD
He's broken my heart in so many pieces, but despite it all I forgive and forget like no tomorrow guaranteed
He is my seed, my rock, my wisdom, my truth and...

(My 1ˢᵗ Love cont'd)

Although, I was young and naïve I understood the word LOVE and I loved HARD…
…it's funny that its 10 years later and I still LOVE you

<u>I use to love you</u>

I use to love you and I still do
Like love and basketball with years in between us
My feelings as fresh as day one
Energy bold and longing to yearn for you
To have you as mine just as before only to never let you go this time
I use to love you and I still do

You were my world and no one could come between that
I have desired no other man but you
My loyalty lies within your hands
Take me as I am with no regrets but to have and to hold…
Please take my hand in marriage one day
See, I use to love you and I still do

I want to nourish and take care of you
While we grow old and plant seeds of wisdom
Just say I do…
…only say it with no regrets

Questions

Where did time go?
Why did you leave?
You said you'd love me to the end and I believed you
Well I'm still here yet you deny my existence and hate my presence
I can see through all that and my intuitions say you still love and desire me just as I do you
But…

Where did time go?
Why did you leave?
Only never to return and to loose contact at your convenience
It's like a thief in the night came and stole my dream, my life…
only you were suppose to protect me
My life has been twisted and knotted because of your absence

Where did time go?
Why did you leave?
Well wherever it went I want you to come back to me
Let's recap and rekindle the flame that hasn't completely died out
by starting over again and promising to take care of us

Unpredictable

Foreshadowing thoughts while patiently awaiting your call……Hey, don't you remember me? We spent our time taking long walks and talks in the park. Yet my nerves jitter more and more each day from the thought of your phone call. You were always unpredictable yet I felt like I could read your heart. Do I still have it? Do you still care? My desire to tell you everything I can. Not to win you over but to inform you of how I feel. We shared our dreams both good and bad. I watched you weep when no one cared. Your energy, your smile, goatee shimmering with bright bold eyes you looked surprised but why? I have always been there loving you, accepting you, and wanting you like the woman I was suppose to be. Yet you've always been so unpredictable…but why were you that way with me? I am your woman, your joy, your all; free yourself within me so that we can see clearer.

Unexpected Catch

Looking into a mirror with a reflection so unique
An image not so perfect and very incomplete
Joys internal and fears embedded
My connection glued tight
Spirits move and become my balance
Internal flutters with moments of silence
Fear of not being able to come correct
But giving my best with who I am
My love flat lines while awaiting resuscitation
My heart opened to be embraced
By the pleasures and experiences that life can bring
With the good that I can share without a diamond ring
It's genuine unlike most and everlasting through the storms
It is what I have
                It is all that I am
                              It is ME

Remembering

In my journey of trusting, learning, loving, and living I have learned an extreme amount of new things to live by. Life is short and full of options. My trust is limited and my heart is slightly scarred. I don't feel bitter but my relationships appear to be unsuccessful. I wonder if it is because my love for this person is never dying. I have learned that life goes on and is hard in all aspects of growth. I have moved and progressed slowly yet I am missing something. My heart is empty and I know not what it lacks. I love some but not completely. I have loved hard and I have loved softly but most of all I have loved. I have been in love once and I am still in love now. I am living alone and soulfully in my mind. I have no desire to start something that I won't finish. I want my life back, I want to love again, and I want to love you. I want to live happily ever after with a family or a child. I want someone or something special and I want to be reminded of the good times, the feelings I use to know, the ones I use to love……I want to remember

Life's interruptions help determine our growth. A prayer can be the difference between happiness and depression. Guilt can consume one's thoughts. Our past should be left behind and our feelings should be respected. Our troubles may come in abundance like our fears yet we have the opportunity to ruin or create our new beginnings.

Life's interruptions help determine our strengths. The many things that put you under are the same things that get you through. When we know who we are our strengths are multiplied by the man above. He gives us all what we need to get by. Our bitterness and extended ego's emancipate self-identity; our bitterness and lack of emancipates self-worth.

Life's interruptions helped determine my growth allowing me to rise above all barriers and obstacles interfering; giving me strength and knowledge about believing in myself. Those interruptions have caused me tears, heart aches, and joy. Yet I still stand strong for those same interruptions helped develop me they gave me my new beginning.

My life's interruptions have been all in good favor and for that I respect who I am today

What We Are

I am
All that I am
Because I believe in us
Determined to be different
Understanding that times have changed
Loving you forever even if it's in my heart
Joining you as one
Announcing to the world what a great man you are
Being able to comfort you when you are weak
Beautiful creation
All that you can be
Reconciling our past differences for a better future

The joy of finding the one you love and wanting to hold on to them forever, goes beyond any bad time that existed. You will always be the only love for me

Soul Mates

I believe that love conquers all
I believe that love conquers all
Because the reality goes beyond the pro's and cons
It is what is embedded from within
It is the seed that GOD plants at birth
It's the bird's sweet melodies
It's the happiness within

I believe that love conquers all
Because true existence never fails
It is the appreciation of availability
Despite the fact that we can't be friends
It is the emotions that no other can give you
For the sake of completion
It is your lost cause

I believe that love conquers all because
when I met you it was love at first sight

I believe that love conquers all
because we never gave up
We had goals and dreams together that are still unmet
Yet we find a way…a way to
Reignite a flame ever burning

I believe that love conquers all and
I believe that since I met you

I've believed
I not only love you
but I believe in you
Time ends

Cont'd

Short comings fall shorter
Loving you has stopped like the time which is continuous
What is going on?
Why are you here?
My love never met you and your facade proved to be untrustworthy
Not afraid of love and I don't want to be rejected
but times are hard and my love is too real
…… to real for bullshit

Untitled

On a midnight summers dream my eyes touched the moonlight
Respect given to the Heavens above
Darkness disguised by stars so bright
Midnight wonders oooohhh what a night
Matching memories with skin so soft
Tingles emerge with every stroke
The moonlight lifted I heard the birds voice
singing and chirping as darkness fell
My energy exploded
Sweet images of God's creation appeared

You know I sometimes ask is this world coming to an end, lets rethink the turn of events.
There's the drunks, drug addicts, dead beat daddy's, the pedophiles, hoe hoppers and feral children who don't have it...a chance to say no please don't hurt me or no please don't leave me because I just want to be loved. Then there's the drug dealers, politicians, and those who don't give a damn what happens to many. Models gone bad and treats for tricks even when hoes are becoming housewives hhhhmmmmmhh (*now ain't that some shyt*) and you ask is this world coming to an end. Well as clear as I can see it...it is the end without a new beginning no voice, no choice of decision making because we are destined to be just as the white man perceives us to be. The belligerent and the ignorant, I want my race to gain in life but they steal and manipulate to get ahead. Quick to holler the white man is holding me back well you tell me is the world coming to an end. For the end is just the beginning and some still have no place to go.

Betrayal

Suspicion, denial, lies, and deceit
All the qualities that I defined regarding you
Remarks out of control, looks vehement, trust bonds broken
I have nil to give
Culminating peaks of anger and frustration
What are my outlets?
Can I break away from this anomaly without loosing my cool?
For I do not want to step outside of my body for the sake of a devils advocate
Nor do I want to forsake the love that I have for myself
For my worth is higher than any of the stupidity that your betrayal has to offer

Incomplete

My soul rested in your hands
My life I thought was all I had
I embraced the memories of you and I
and now it's hard to say good bye
To all the love and some of the hate
Lingering arguments that couldn't wait
The home we had was definitely real
but now you're gone and it sits still
With hopes and dreams of you coming home
Are you lost or have you intentionally gone away?

The Color of Love

Grey and White pallets turned Blue
Bursting smells intrigue my nose.
The sight of laughter fills the sky
Embrace the happiness
Enjoy the moment
My color of love is Grey
for it has no definition, shape, or guarantee
My color of love is Comfortable and wonderfully complete

Interpersonal relationships destroyed
Insecurity and lack of confidence in self
Predetermination to be a failed character
No commitment with whom I am suppose to be
My trust for others far fetched
My emotions barely existing
My soul dangles from a tree
like loose limbs awaiting their final death
Uprooted from within there is nothing remaining…
…I am empty

Deciding to date

I denied myself the right to live
I denied myself the right to love

Figuring aimlessly how the world turns
Wondering about each episode

Looking into a vision that may never come true
Imagining my life with you

Uncertainties soaring…afraid to try
Because maybe it will repeat itself since the last time I tried

Unforgiving to myself at times…my spirit has died
Happiness probably a step away

Hoping that I live day to day
Wanting to be strong and tall

Wishing for my day to come…
Imagining my life complete

Imagining life without defeat

I have given myself a chance to breathe again

I can now see

Bad timing (Scrambled thoughts)

Missing chances to take advantage of you
Opportunities passing for me to talk to you
Not aware of my inner wants vs. what's best for me
Bad timing allowed me to walk away from me
A connection as genuine as leather, whipped past me silently
Now I have screwed that up and probably many more to come
My fears and lack of trust allows me to miss out many possible opportunities
I guess bad timing won't be for the moment

Demeaning standards
Impatient views
Undesirable undertones
Most of my thoughts of you
Self respect lacking with the current times
Listening to your voice with nothing but lies
Lies to deceive everyone but self…

Now did you believe it?
Were you serious??

Tables turned your bullshit flowing
Circling your thoughts playing with your mind
Is it enough…hardly, I sigh
Defeating yourself at your own game
Looking with a pitiful face…oh what a shame

Demeaning my standards
Having inpatient views
Those undesirable undertones
Gave me my initial point of view about you
Now nothing has changed
My heart still guarded by one less…
Bullshitter that the game has to offer

The power of love

Love is something ever changing and ever flowing
The melodies you hear on a sweet sunny day
The bitterness you taste when you are sick to your stomach

Love can bring about change in many kinds
From your worst enemies to your greatest lovers of all times
It is the difference between a one night stand and a lifetime complete
It is the yearning that I feel when you reach out to me
My inner soul burning with fiery flames as hot as lava
The craving that becomes a must
It is the everlasting connection that exist beyond the end

Love is something ever changing and ever flowing
The melodies you hear on a sweet sunny day
The bitterness you taste when you are sick to your stomach

The anger you feel through turmoil
It's the murder you commit with each slash of the tongue
The tattoo you got and now regret
The child support never filed
All the time given… that was the initial question from the start
The day they left you with a broken heart

See yall for me…
The power of love is the shit that can wake you and can break you every single day

Stress of disbelief
Wonders of what is next
Turmoil soaring at the thought of repetition
Attempts to recover the original piece…
…the piece that brought us together initially
Where do we go from here?
Concerns and pleas for clarity
Mentally challenged by the future
My first mind is to escape from the locks that bind me to this world
The pain that must be endured from life to death
The pleasure that should be enjoyed along the way
Where is the fun

A night altered by the summer air
As the winds softly drift across my face
I sigh and close my eyes to imagine the touch
Inhaling the purity that nature has to offer
The sounds of the night creatures pleasant as the sky
The stars high and still just as the oceans tide
Refreshing breeze embrace my memories
Reminiscing about those loved one's from my past
Exhaling at what is only a dream
Emptiness takes over and hollow holes fill with tears…
…as that memory has become my reality

Desperation unclear
Options limited, why the impatience
See you hold the recipe book but can't seem to understand it
My preferences clear and unmet through the eyes of expectations
Yet you hound me as though I owe you
Owe you for what was never mistaken
You desired me when you wanted your wants and needs to be fulfilled
All at the sound of your drum
Your patience short and no tolerance of my delays
But ask yourself...
How long have I waited ... 1000 plus days?
Just for you to discover womanhood
How selfish and undeserving were you of my time, wants, and needs

Rejection of self
Denial of rights
High demands of lies
Honesty non-fulfilling
Pleasure unsatisfactory
Whining moments of uncertainty
Feelings of realness
Emotions at an all time low
So tired of people and their ideas for me
I love, I care, I breathe, and I listen
even with rejection of self-acceptance

Denial of rights to be me
High demands for lies to satisfy self
Honesty non-fulfilling for fear of heart break
Pleasure unsatisfactory for selfish desires
Whining moments of uncertainty and in the end
...I'm still the same person
I commit myself to knowledge
I breathe the same air as you
I am me and that's all that should matter

Bullshit

Immaturity, ignorance, disgrace, and disgust is what you've left for me to think of you
A lie with no remorse of the looseness of your tongue
The pity expected from those around you because of all the things you've done
Unbroken promises and unfulfilled commitments only allow me to think of
...dead ends and cul-de-sacs because you can't through them
You see no wrong in what you do
You listen to nothing but speak so fast
You're an accident waiting to occur and hopefully the impact will bring you back
...back to reality because realistically speaking
You've headed down the wrong path and I'm NOT going with you

Get it together

Some fight for freedom to love, live, and let die. To engage in the change of the unjust favors of the world for better pay, housing, and life. For the right to believe how ever they may want.

Some fight for freedom to not be forced into a gang. To stay in school so they can maintain…stability in life with liberty and justice forever is what they say. The strength to grow strong and have people in their lives to hold on to because where they came from that's all that they can do.

Some fight for freedom to believe that life is all we have and education is all we can get. I fight for freedom to save the world from the lurking dangers that are hidden behind doors. Freedom to teach the world that has gone astray. To the underlying hands of men who make promises to love you in all the wrong ways.

Some fight for freedom because they have no choices. I fight for freedom because it's my voice. Let's change the outcomes in the world today.

Sisterhood

Is not controlling
  Demanding
  Obsessive
  Jealous

  It does not require Prying
    Pre-Judgments
    Too much energy
    Competition

    But it does take Trust
      Honesty
      True Love
      Commitments

To be my sister you must commit to sisterhood and see me just as I see you…we must be on a level where we can see eye to eye…individually! Sisterhood takes time to grow and a second to tear it apart…

Now ask yourself, do you really want to be my sister?

My expectations of my sister…
Would be to have a lending hand, a listening ear. To have an open heart and a free soul. To respect my decisions and my lifestyle as mine. To rejoice at my happiness and to emit nothing but joy. To emulate what a real sister would be like. To catch my tears when they fall and hold my head when hung. To sing the songs we learned together…to be nothing less than my sister

The life of the abnormal is no more than the life of the non-existent
Misunderstood, misguided, and misused from the task of wanting to fit in
Why can't I function like everyone else???
My sex drive, thought processes, lack of interest, etc...
Where does normalcy lie?
Why does society have the right to define what's right?
If my head hurts from thoughts then imagine how my heart feels...
I am normal and fucked up all in one
But the question is can you handle me in both stages of my life

How can I begin to know, if I'm not allowed to grow
But how can I grow if I don't understand the way things occur…

Is it my confusion or yours?
Where and/or what lies in your head?
What are you thoughts?
How do you view yourself?
In what ways can we benefit each other?

When signs are showed what do they mean?
Do you stop in the midst of your current plans to redirect your thought?

How do you let go of the not so obvious for total confusion and darkness?
Well nothing is guaranteed and everything that has potential should be sought out with care

So go ahead and step out on faith
Because what we see may be our wants and what we need HE knows we don't need…

So Stuck

The pain in my ass

How can I be honest with you when all you want are lies?
How can you question me and act as though my responses are surprises
Are you ready for a person like me?
Or does your lustful soul allow misinterpretation in your mind
I give you the benefit of doubt but mostly all the time I'm proven wrong
Where is the maturity that you proclaimed?
Or is it just as desirable as your wants
You speak about the future but continuously overlook the present
You sell yourself dreams
Yet I'm so full of laughter at the ignorance and denial that I try to take you from…
…but that's impossible too
You speak highly as if your thoughts and views are solid
but let me be the first to say your shyt is as liquefied as boiling water…
Boiling water which represents the temperature I feel after having an immature conversation based on assumptions with you

                Somebody anybody help her…

God knows best and God seeks out the good

Things through Christ

Jesus is your partner through your long walk in life. He is all that you need your light, strength, and guidance. Trust in Him, live by Him, and believe in Him. God will show you the way. To understanding why we live, learn, and love is to understand……………………
why we die…nobody knows.

Temptation takes over our minds and fear takes over our bodies. Physically we respond like scared babies. Mentally we do what society feels is correct when neither is right nor wrong. Where is one to look for the right answer? Where do we turn for our knowledge? God knows, He sees, speaks and determines but we must seek out the answers through our pastors, teachers, leaders, high powers, etc…Don't be misguided forever, there is a right turn and a wrong turn.

Blessed is he who trust in the Lord
Blessed is he who has faith in the Lord
Blessed is he who believes GOD will deliver him
We are all blessed as individuals in our own way

<u>A day to remember</u>

I watched you leave
I watched you leave
Without one word of goodbye
Wanting to hold no fault to the current circumstances

I watched you leave
With tears in my eyes and weights on my heart
Knowing I gave my heart to you but it wasn't enough
No eye contact or stutter in your thoughts…
You Ok'd my decisions as if they were your wants

I watched you leave with a life lesson learned
…only if that moment could have come before I watched **<u>YOU LEAVE</u>**

I watched you leave and now you're not looking back…and I don't want to move forward
but what do we do…what do I do?

But watch you leave and know that I'll always love you

Who I am

Destiny denied a game playing repeatedly in my mind and never ending. Am I a lost cause? Forgiven by many but still misunderstood. Will I be rejected? Unsure of my future and haunted by my past. Questions of my allowance. Unforgettable memories affect my present times. Have I really changed for the better? Wants of invisibleness, wishing people would forget about me… Thoughts of hatred and lack of being. I refuse to believe it but how do you erase truth? I must stop fighting me but my internal memories persuade my future

Is it too good to be true?

The connection that existed was one that I didn't believe could. It came from out of no where, it seemed so misunderstood. The thought that it can last is unclear in my mind for I had not yet ventured into that straight side where women seek curiosity and I am the prey. Sought out for an experience and ready to play…to play with my feelings though she says that hers are true. Her line was "I never thought that I could be attracted to you"

The connection that existed was one that I didn't believe could. Well things happen and stuff doesn't go your way sometimes. I know that because it's the same reaction that is happening with mine. But how could I receive you're straight as an arrow on a crooked bow but the sensation is sought first then mentally we'll grow…grow on each other to learn what's real. Maybe you will see you don't need a man for that same feeling. For I have all that you need in a package complete.

The connection that existed was one that I didn't believe could. I was unsure if it was a "for now" fling but the connection that I doubted worked out just fine.

An African Child

An African child has smiles so bright
A sweet soft voice that whispers at night
The sound of a voice so fair with winds blowing and the moons bright glare
She speaks with lips like plums, the curl and the rolling of her tongue
To say to those "***mime cha kwa we***" (I come unto you) in Swahili

An African child has smiles so wide with open arms and big brown eyes
Her sway, her switch so sassy and proud
Her lengthy locks
Her knit tight brows
This African child of color so sweet
Is like a warm bath to make your night complete.

S/N: Beauty starts from within, take advantage of your inner spirits and allow them to be your guide

Why

After all the times you hurt me
The times you made me cry
Why do I forgive you?
With every little sigh
The times you betrayed me
And the times of painful goodbyes
Why do I feel I still need you?
After all those lies
The times you ignored me
And the times my pain has shown
Why do I still care for you?
Though you left me all alone
With the scars you left upon me
And the tears that fall each day
Why am I still in love with you?
Though you treated me this way

Love Calls

Images surrounding the sweet summer sky
Like birds chirping in the trees so high
Songs in my ear while your smile takes over my sight
I am feeling the vibes from your warm soul
I am learning to connect with you sensuality
I am receiving your energy
You speak to me softly and my imagination runs
You touch me gently, it makes my heart murmur
I have connected with you
And I am feeling love…

Random thought:

Why does the sound of rain break through the air so high and every drop dripped is tears from God's eye. When sands blow and mountains moves; there are rivers flowing and nature's growing awaiting spring bloom

The images of beauty lie in open fields while the suns rays feed them energy
Multitudes of colors and smells drifting from the plants wonders
Hidden secrets lie below the surface and the dirt continues to nourish the root for outside beauty

When nature calls its an awakening moment that is interesting to watch just as the creation of life starts as an egg and develops into a wonderful being……an interesting exchange

Inner city crisis

Inner city blues whispers above the cold midnight air with kids on the street corners and trash everywhere. Pimps and hoes, buses and trains, street lingo calls for everybody's name.

Inner city blues whispers above the cold midnight air. People dancing to the moon light even when no one's there. To watch them twirl and sing out loud. The only two things they can do to feel proud. Proud of who they are and where they've come from.

Inner city blues have cries for help. Inner city blues is some last steps… steps toward freedom or insanity, work or the penitentiary. Inner city blues is definitely what it is. Inner city blues is also what's real. No need to fake or front, no need to sigh.

Inner city blues is where I come from that's why we see eye to eye…

S/N: respect where you come from and you will learn to appreciate where you are going

One bad habit

Love can be like a musical
The sweet sound of love making in the air
It can be the peace after a late night affair
To have and to hold that one good thing that makes your heart sing
Where did my inspiration go…?
What made everything end?
That one bad habit that you couldn't shake
That one bad habit that just couldn't wait
For better or worse to death do you part?
That one bad habit that broke your heart into pieces so very small
Now your world has fallen apart
To mend and sew it back together almost seems impossible
Chances are slim but the urge to change isn't enough
with it being half the key to your happiness
Patience is a virtue but when it's your habit "tu no entiendo mi pensamiento"
(You don't understand my thoughts)
It's a matter of self realization…
…and that won't happen anytime soon
                    Incomplete…

When a good relationship is taken over by one's introduction to drugs know that it is not your fault and there is nothing that you can do…but shed one last tear

Juices

Strawberry, cherry, or banana flavor savoring my mouths salivary glands
The moisture overtakes my senses and pulls me closer to the objects
The taste touches my tongue and my heart quivers
Moisture burst into an overflowing river
The taste ignites my moisture *(Oh my)*
How my heart races to get to the middle from which these flavors flow
Seeking the need, wanting more
To taste these flavors I cannot lie…
Makes my shyt thump harder
I began to sigh…
I come back for seconds and your head drops back
You open your legs so that I may explore this overflowing river once more
I taste you, you taste so sweet
I taste strawberry, cherry, and banana treats.

Untitled Political thoughts

My goals, my dreams, my future ahead. My journey of dead ends and blurred vision. The fights and battles to claim my status…as I emerge. I am a no body in a crowd of many. Where do I turn? Who do I trust? MYSELF!!!! How can I when I am my biggest enemy. Now I envision the world as a comfort place to all. I envision the world to be an abundance of opportunity.

Yet my goals, my dreams, my future ahead ends with blurred vision and an over strained head. The determination is high but my opportunity low and with no where to go with all my goals and my dreams…I am still that nobody in a crowd of many…persecuted by the hands of the law makers now who will improve my future?

Greek Life

Greek life has been above and beyond the most challenging experience in my life outside of some of my own personal troubles. Nonetheless overall I've grown in patience still advancing in trust but each different obstacle has been a stepping stone for me. It has its moments to where you might wanna say fuck this shyt but it also makes you not want to give up because of self assurance. An identity was created that help reveal the true strengths and weaknesses of me. You create bonds with some that will never end. New friends well new family…people to appreciate. Giving back to the communities and standing up for your beliefs were the best part. Having a mission statement and values that match your beliefs. The idea that many before you have paved the way and contributed to the community and some times the world. The idea of a never ending bond or eternal sisterhood sounds great. However human beings functions in all of these parts and human beings have different personalities, personal beliefs, cognitive patterns, and ideas of what it should be like. So I say unto you do your research, choose wisely and don't be in a hurry to decide because the Greek life can make or break you and all sisterhoods aren't real!!!! Greek life experience was my ultimate challenge of the year…

Introducing Soror Lost and Found b.k.a Special Ed, Beta Gamma Chapter, summer 2004

<u>A Mother</u>

A mother in so many words is your ultimate energy. It is she who gives you the strength to do all things. It is she that molds you to be the person you are today. The touch of her hand and the sound of her voice helps steer you through hard times. It is the comfort in knowing that she is there. The comfort that is imperative for positive bonding at birth till about three…the comfort that is necessary even when they are disappointed in you.

A mother's love is not just a mother's love it's a stow-away for our inner feelings. It's a diary with no key. It's a best friends deepest secret. It's our inner peace. It's the person you look to, to hear everything will be okay even if you made a bad decision. It's the backbone that should be available to lean on when you your world has fallen apart. So to my mother along with everyone else's you all are so dear to me… I say thank you for giving me strong parts of you and I take those parts of you with me forever.

Intimate Moments

The intimate moments we share are like the moments you take out to shave or groom your hair
It's personal yet so pleasant
I go deeper
Although hesitant to my carefulness… it is what completes you
Precision and determination is what makes you cum
Harder and harder you moan from within…
To the feelings of intensity, it is the shyt that makes your heart beat and your legs tremble
You mumble for more and more
You thrive for this piece of me that doesn't really exist …
Only if I could feel you myself how sweet it would be
Although a mental image connects my emotions
I feel you from within…and I cum
Now we share the same intimate moment

For what its worth

When I awake in the morning sometimes there's sun sometimes there's rain.
When I look into the eyes that lie next to me sometimes I feel pain
So sorry at times for everything I've done, for who I am…hell sometimes for all the above
But for what its worth whether you like, hate, or love me my life goes on…
I can say that now even though I may hurt inside
Because when I lay to sleep at night God is by my side…
To allow me to wake up tomorrow to more sun or rain…
…whether there is love or there is pain
Regardless, if I like or hate my inner self at times
It's a constant battle that keeps me alive
When I think about ending it all God keeps calling my name
To say to me, my daughter be strong life goes on and a blessed one you will have
Fuck those who do you wrong

It belongs to me

My gain is and will be your loss because my gain is for me, whether you know it or not
To await my gain is to loose yourself and too loose yourself is to loose your mind
Your body and your soul goes too
By playing the game of awaiting my gain, is to play yourself and have less than you've already loss

S/N: Finding yourself through your experiences is the best thing you can do. To live your life through someone else is absolutely ridiculous for both.

Sleepless Nights

As I lay here awake I hear the sounds of birds chirping, sound of snoring, no one whoring but choked up engines, brakes squeaking and lovers quarrelling…what will be the outcome. For nights at a time I lie awake before dawn. No thoughts racing but the outside world still existing, what will be the outcome of the society we live in? Our brothers and mothers…where and who will they turn to for guidance.

As I lay here awake I hear the sounds of the birds chirping, sound of snoring, but no one whoring just choked up engines, brakes squeaking, and two lovers quarrelling one saying kill me as the other says call for help…my heart …but baby for real my heart. As I lie here awake at night, my sleepless nights will be the cause of my restless days.

Still Standing

YOU took it
The one thing that was so precious to me
YOU took it
As if it meant nothing to you
YOU took it

You took it and left me empty on the inside
and searching to find my way
A piece of me that was to be embraced
and welcomed when the time was right yet...
YOU took it

Without permission a interaction so explicit
Your mind fucked obviously to the possibility
of what could become of me
Yet, YOU STILL TOOK IT

Lost and Confused
Abandoned and Misused...
I questioned life
The outcome silenced and never repeated
or heard of till 23 years later...
YOU took it...and never once cared about the damage you caused
Yet I did my best to remain strong through it all

No outlet for comfort just my little secret
Eating away at me at times
Never allowing me to be comfortable to those who cared

Mentally disconnected with the perfect facade
Life on an emotional rollercoaster...All because YOU took it from me
I have flat lined but ....Karma will be your BITCH!!!

Back at it again

A good thing gone bad that's what I once thought
Love as prominent as before...
Where do we start? Where do we go from here?
Unanswered questions and thought patterns changed
Growth matured but can it last or hold things together
Back at it again for what round 2, 3, or 4, with one thing for sure
and the love still as prominent as before
The look in your eyes
The passion behind your smile
The beat in your heart reassures me that...
the love never stopped

Self Sabotage

How do I continue on when my strength is failing? The energy once applied is dying without guilt. My words unheard. My notions unseen. My heart already heavy and broken with the pieces getting smaller each day. Do you see me for who I am or just another closed chapter in your book called life.

Holding on to merely nothing but strands, the tension on each loosens as though you are awaiting me to fall. Just let go and let me be free…free from your puppetry. Lately each move has been on you.

How do I continue on when my strength is failing and the energy once applied is dying without guilt? I deserve a full time lover and friend not the pencil you in and play at my convenience type of love.

Ask yourself, what are you not willing to loose?

Tiring and exhausting images enter my mind
A mental capacity once clear now fills with clouded jaded images
The purity of my vision tainted
A memory once pleasant has left a bitter taste in my mouth
A taste so unwanted that it burns my esophagus entirely
When will it fade?
When time eases over and the sun shines again
Although mentally I can see through this difficult moment
It is uneasy in my mind
Wanting to reach my goals
and determined to succeed
I must see past the tainted image that was left of you

Holiday joys and Holiday tears Donny Hathaway's "This Christmas" playing loudly in my ear. Ground covered with snow while the trees stand tall. Enjoying the beauty of it all. A hard holiday to handle yet my favorite of all. The music brings peace to my lonely heart. A heart that desires to share the family happiness in the air…while Boys II Men's "Let it snow" soothes my mind…still there are others that leave behind the memories of those not near for Holiday joys and Holiday tears. Enjoy each moment with those who are dear to your heart. Because some get snatched too soon and nothing remains but a memory that never fades. A memory not quite the same as the presence of that being.

Questioning the trust forms of sisterhood

An image blurred by misconception and disbelief. The idea of forming lasting bonds with some people who are judgmental and insecure of themselves in the forefront of my mind. What is it again that we have in common?
…Oh, solemnly the idea of coming together and being apart of something greater than ourselves. Ourselves exactly, the 1st and last person we think about each day…
And the person that no matter how many times you call me your sister, you carry a deeper envy for …not in a jealous way because some just can't shake the self-centeredness……
…but I understand
An image blurred by misconception and disbelief… so fucked up that even the trust built within that sisterhood couldn't change it…

Untitled

Look into my eyes…what do you see?
Listen with your ears…what do you hear?
Now look from within my eyes and listen with my ears…
You didn't know that I was real
You couldn't hear me on the outside because you prejudged me
I exist in many ways other than what you see
I have a cry for help, hell I have my own plea
Just because I'm slightly different from you in less ways than you choose to believe
If you open your eyes and listen a little bit more carefully
you too will have a plea…
Everyone should be learned from within before they are prejudged from the out
You never know who you're encountering and will be without

Opening Eyes

I woke up this morning to find my arm reaching for you, and you weren't there to reach back. I've heard of this before but never really experienced it. I asked myself are these just feelings that came about since this morning and when I had no response I wondered was this the way I felt but hadn't been comfortable enough to share with anyone not even myself.

To yearn for a love so strong and real, the inner reality consuming your make beliefs, you dig deeper to learn about the true you. To let go of yourself and breath in deeper. Your heart aches for more…more passion than you've had ever existed is exhaled. You are now free… free to explore what's been on your mind. Comfortable enough to let the feelings come from behind, letting go of a mask held up for so long. You yearn for the touch, the passion, the love, that you can share. The love so strong and real… the only way to feel. Like giving back is what its worth and receiving the affection that you once dreamed, you awaken to the scare of sensuality. You are accepting the true you and you now have sight.

Taking a turn

Life's challenge is the ultimate way for seeking wisdom. God is first and foremost for life's answer but through blessings from him above we find life long partners for whom we share our inner most thoughts; our lives, love, and our understanding of what things mean to us. Challenges come about at early ages whether it's a relationship between a parent and a child that has ended in abandonment, abuse, molestation, or even a broken heart. It is all something that must be overcome. It definitely won't be easy and no situation will be different from any other. The absence of love is the final result of all situations. Finding love is a yearning for all individuals of all ages and when the time comes it will be revealed unto you. It will be suited for your needs accept it; work with it for it will be difficult at times because it will be all you know. You will hurt still and be challenged but pray and work through it until all of the right answers are revealed unto you. For we are God's children and he only gives us so much to bear but you must know when to let go and when to hold on for finding the right one and letting go of the old is a start of making a turn for the better.

It's worth it

Continuous disappointments and confrontation with no clarification
Unexplained reasons for action
The taste in my mouth
My reactions
Explosive energy building within
Wanting to release the pressure in the most pleasant manner
All awaiting opportunities would only give off negative energy
Self pleasure a must
Blood boiling within my veins like a volcano awaiting its day to erupt
Attempting to keep cool *para no neccesito ser enojado (because it's not necessary to be mad)*
Impressions on a sliding scale downward
Experience enough and unwanted
Tired of the failures presented to me

My heart

I imagined you again in a dream so pure and wonderful
Your request for me came alive
The laughter and motion…a dream come true
As I opened my eyes to a breaking sweat
The reality came back to me
I lie alone in my bed…with just a thought of you

Costa Rica

A sky so beautiful when clouds don't touch. Many different colors and types of people all sharing a common way of living and that is in harmony. Food very different and versatile. *Ticos fuerme moto (people smoking weed)* and dance bars open all night. Wonderful bliss of Samaron welcomes me. Police patrol street with no real jobs, everything legal at the age 18 including driving. Heredia *es la cuidad en San Jose Costa Rica* with loud streets and many cars. Not quite like the beach but more my style. Better selections and a bigger crowd. Many stores with normal things to do but if I has to sum up Costa Rica you'll drink till you're Blue

How I see myself

Body image distorted
Seeing more fat and rolls than normal
Uncertain about my figure
Since my early childhood years
Always taunted about being too thin
Weighing in at 125 around 17

Are you depressed?
Do you eat?

Never suffering from anorexia nor bulimia
Just family pressures to not get big
Now I'm 155 at age 25 and all they can say is…
…"if you don't slow down you gonna be big as a house"
Standing 5'8" with absolutely no weight
My mind continues to stress about my desires to be thin

What size will I be in my future life to come?
Never wanting a child for fear of getting large and not being able to shake it
Uncertain of my figure and my true image
I grow more uncomfortable…
Never being able to look in the mirror

My intimate moments semi-dressed and concealed by total darkness
Wondering am I desirable to my mate
Body image distorted
Seeing more fat than normal
Is it a figment of my imagination?
Or am I really fat?

Mister G

He beat me for no reason
Seemingly every chance he would get
He beat me just because…I couldn't defend myself
He beat for moving to slow
He beat me when I got an average grade
He yelled so much when my mom wasn't home
I can remember being so afraid…
Afraid of what reason would be next
…Until I realized I didn't need one
He'd say it's for the better
Did he hate me?
Is my mom gonna ever leave?
Can someone help me?
I hated him with every breath I had, I hated him
How could a child have so much internal rage for a man that's not even my Dad?
…I'm reminded he wasn't my choice
My family questioned if he touched me? What is he doing?
I honestly don't know…I don't remember if anything past being hit happened
but I hated to be alone with him because I knew he would beat me more
Each whipping left whelp marks
I remember the burning sensation that my hand rubs could never soothe
Increasing my fear and trust in people
I hated the idea of who or what would be next
For at least three years of my life this was my memory
Uncertain of the actual number just wanting to forget…
Unable to forgive and…in the back of my mind with each beating I could KILL
KILL him for how he destroyed a piece of my spirit
KILL him for contributing to my issues as if there wasn't enough
She gets under my skin and I can't help but feel the irritation
Like a deep sting from a bees bite

(Mister G Cont'd)

The continuous itch you can never seem to satisfy
The pain you get over time its still swelling
Nothing can soothe it but I wonder when it will stop
When will the initial reaction begin to reverse?
When will the pain stop getting worse
When will that irritation reduce itself and become more pleasant
When…can I count on things to become better?
Knowing how life and human beings work probably…
…NEVER

What's going on?

What's going on…I mean got damn…what's going on
I feel trapped in my mind
It's like I'm in an insane asylum
Confused and delusional with a few out to get me
My head hurts from the frustration and irritation that I'm experiencing

What's going on…I mean damn…what's going on
It's like one issue to the next this shit never seems to end
Is it that serious when we are only friends?
Aggravation should not exist or is this a test of my patience

What's going on…I mean damn…what's going on
Feelings of wanting to run away and escape what seems to be a nightmare
Does it end?
Will it ever stop?
I can't take it anymore
I would rather my heart stop

Realistically

When do you begin to realize that men ain't shit?
When do you begin to see that he's feeding you more than just his dick?
Your mind seems to be as shallow as a clear water pond
With your eyes shut tight and your heart wide open you become your biggest enemy
Why?
Because you'll lie to yourself just to feel what seems to be good…
You'll stab yourself in the back to cover your true feelings
How rude
So to you I say when do you begin to realize that you should expect more and tolerate less
When do begin to realize that you are all you need to caress your ego and stroke that low self esteem
Shall I continue…?
I think not, because I've concluded that you'll begin to realize that life isn't going to wait for you to catch up to it…it will only pass you by
Just like that man…so hold your ground and realize that your pussy is coated with a shield of armor that gold just like your heart should be
Only let in what you can handle and let go of what will weigh you down
So now my question to you is…
When will you begin to realize that you are all you need?
And you must love yourself first

In over my head

Sometimes I get in a zone
Unexpectedly it seems when all is going wrong
Being alone has become important to me
Wanting to break loose
Wanting to be free
Free because I'm in over my head
Free because no point in wanting to be dead
To let go and be clear of all that confuses my mind
Just to be able to think clearly one damn time

Sometimes I get in a zone
Unexpectedly it seems when all is going wrong
Being alone has become important to me
Wanting to break loose
Wanting to be free
I confess I am nothing more than a mere image trying to see eye to eye
Trying to find my way from the path of unrighteousness
Just to connect to something that's real
Just to be able to feel…
To feel something outside of what's numb
Numb me from feeling
From connecting to something so sweet
I'd give anything to keep from being weak

Please take me out of this zone
Unexpectedly because all went wrong
I no longer want to be alone
Please free me from my boggled mind
I'm in way over my head
Please clear my mind

Yelling I have Pride

I shout that we are all equal
I say that we will remain the same
To our rainbow family
But what is my claim

It means that I a woman, can define myself as I choose to be
It means that I a woman can choose my sexuality
What difference does it make that you view me as immoral
My morality is defined within myself
Fuck your morals

I ride under the six colors that are beautiful to me
The six colors that define our equality
The six colors that keep our families tight
The colors that make us fight for equal right both day and night

For marriage, fairness, and gay awareness you name it
For the opportunity to proclaim it
Just as heterosexuals do
For the benefits that civil unions offer
For the benefits that will be available for our sons and daughters

For the environment that I can share with my mate
For the stupid ass system that loves to hate
To hate on our families because we share pride
Pride so strong it can't be denied
But to understand love, nature and the abilities of the sun
is to understand the healing, spirit, and harmony we share as one…some just don't get it

So I say to you again

I shout that we are all equal
I say that we remain the same
To our rainbow family
Now do you understand my claim?

You're no different than I am
You're no different than us
So why continue to break us apart...
make us all distrust
The system that is suppose to protect but yet it rejects our fabulous six colors that makes us

I shout that we are all equal
I say that we remain the same
To our rainbow family
PLEASE understand our claim

S/N: it shouldn't matter who is lying in my bed. All gays/lesbians are not into conversion. Please know that straight people hit on gays and their existence alone is not enough to hold them at fault......Wake up people and accept responsibility for your actions and yours alone.

SOMETIMES I FEEL THAT I AM STUPID, I HATE MYSELF. I WILL NEVER HAVE A LIFE, I WILL NEVER LOVE AGAIN. I'VE BEEN TOLD I AM A FAILURE SO FAR IT SEEMS THAT I HAVEN'T PROVED ANY OF THEM WRONG. I HATE MY INNER SOUL, I HATE MYSELF, I HATE THAT I WAS BORN, I HATE WHO I AM, I HATE THE FACT OF WHO I AM NOT, I HATE THAT I HATE, I HATE BEING ALIVE DEATH WOULD DO ME JUSTICE, DEATH WILL GIVE ME PEACE. DEATH IS WHAT I'M LOOKING FOR TO GET RID OF STUPID OLE. NO MORE PROBLEMS AND NO MORE FEARS BECAUSE YOU AND I HATE ME BOTH……MAYBE I SHOULD DRIVE OVER A CLIFF, DROWN IN SEA, STABB MYSELF AND WATCH THE BLOOD RUN……

S/n: On this day I must have had an extreme amount of pain going on. There are various scribbles and marks throughout the paper as if I was digging my pen into it. Let's just say I am thankful that I am not in that space anymore…

What do you do?
What choices to make?
Where does my heart wander?
Where does my mind go?
What fantasies can I fulfill?
What loopholes can I explore?
How can we connect?
How can we grow?
When can I see you?
When can I know?
Who has your heart?
Who has your soul?
Why are you so vulnerable for love?
Why don't you know?

Endless Love

One lonely night of a passionate kiss awaits
Your sound with the water and sands drifting
The calls of dolphins mating, is like human flesh
with sweat and water dripping from her beloved bosom
The sweet ecstasy that is delivered
The love that I receive from when you call out my name
The gripping kisses that flow around my body makes me shiver
The time we spend is not what matters
Yet the love we share is what's real
Do you believe that you have reached your destiny?
Have you yet to climax
Have you yet to dream
With sweet thoughts flowing through your inner mind
Your soul releases itself
Your body shakes and quivers to the soft touches of my tongue
Yet you desire more
You desire the completeness from within
so I search to fill your emptiness with my warm spirit
Upon entrance you embrace the sun rays and beauty shimmers
The look on your face is so pleasant
So sweet, the love we made is now complete
We see the moons glare above the still waters
We hear the motionless air across the sea
We lie here exhausted while receiving the moment that drift us off to sleep

Untitled

Life has its ways of revealing the unknown
It has many outlets that are hidden
Many secrets untold
Feelings let go, the trampling and tossing of each others thoughts
Emotions soar high
The idea that you will fly away with me and we'll have peace everlasting crushed
Just like the thought of compatibility
See you are who I want you to be rather than being yourself and unfortunately I'm not interested in that
I need more than a faced of innocence for we both know that doesn't exist
The taunting and teasing of nothing being good enough lies ahead
Because you weren't good enough for yourself
I lean and look to you for friendship, love, trust and you seem to lack the true skills of the three…and you say you wanna be with me
Well my love I can't be with you, you are a ticking time bomb waiting to explode and you say you love me
But you have let me in on a secret of yours……….
You like the idea of things being your way, playing with ones feelings and having a picket fence dream
But in actuality you are not ready for someone real, life, or love because you are not ready for yourself…Therefore causing me not to be ready for you
See you have to know you before I can get to know you

Wouldn't you like to know?

My true image goes beyond what you can see
It is not something for you to just figure out over night
My true image protects me from harm and never lets me flee
It is what comforts me in the still nights that lie ahead under the dark black sky
It's the shyt that makes you think about me, it's the shyt that makes you sigh
It's the image that you would like to be so clear but it is yet such a funny blur
But you mistake this image as a mistake of my own
Yet this is the image that protects me and never lets me flee
This is the image that awaits the one true real me
and only those who can reveal this image
…are the ones who can understand me…

Language

Language is spoken through art, body, the tongue, and the mind
It is the roll of you body
It is the pulsation against my hand that I adore
The soft movement of the tongue with words so deep, the mentality of the wise and colors so bright
I imagine language to be as beautiful as the sun, and deep as the oceans
I imagine language to consist of many flavors that savor the words like melting ice
I image language to speak to me like soft music that we make love to under the moon light
The words to flow freely and uplift us as a whole
I imagine language to set us free both spiritually and emotionally
I imagine it to consume my every atom and fill my organs so that I may speak in tongues
and love you properly
I imagine language to be my expression of Life
I imagine language to express Love

Confirmation

Confirmation burned my soul into the smallest amount of dust ever
The tears fell from my eyes as my heart raced, puddles began to grow
The fear that my world would come to an end
The very sound of I just didn't know how to tell you replaying in my mind
As the confirmation burned a hole into my soul a new light began to shine
The light revealed a reflection…an image
The image of a beautiful young woman that still has time to grow
………………………….He left and now I must hang dry!!

My world stopped

My world stopped this week, when I thought time was endless
It came crashing down like a Tsunami that connected to land
My world stopped as my heartbeat faded, the end for me is now
I never thought that this would happen to me like this
See…when my world stopped it took all the air and life that I had to give
The energy re-wound itself as it dissipated into darkness
It crushed me…I mean every single bone in my body
It stole the most important thing to me which was <u>HOPE</u>
It laid me to rest and cremated me mentally
When my world stopped so did my *LOVE*

I have searched high and low for you with no known outlets left to explore
My vision clouded with disappointment
The message delivered but to an unknown address
How can I locate thee if the existence is none?
Does your heart search for me?
Can you breathe without me?
Your respirator thriving off my inspiration you inhale Life
A life that was meant to be shared by us two
So, until I find you I'll continue to search high and low for you…
Just keep your hopes high for when I find you…you will be safe

Twice the charm

Disarray and delusions about the future
Your affect flat
Your tone melancholy
Destined to seek the everlasting yet…growth stunted from disbelief
For your thoughts become your actions and your actions are not of my interest peak

Time consuming gestures yet the lack of effort unseen
Truth knotted so tightly that the story goes untold
Imagery that was once a beautiful sight has now become a dark moment
Your heart says one thing but your mind has control

Determined to have only the best
That seeks to enjoy the pleasures of love
That love that rests in a pool of warm water
The love that comforts the soul
Unselfishly and unknowingly real

That love will be…a part of my future
That love will be enjoyable
That love will be for me

What's becoming

Could it be happening all over again or will it end in just a flop of disappointment
Is there a chance for a new start at a fresh heart?
Being able to express myself and communicate my inner pains
Findings…the thing that has never laid itself to rest…how ironic
You still exist like a lonely lily in a field of daises
How do you stand out in front of the rest?
Is it charm or just personality that lifts a weeping tree?
The spirit and joys of happiness ringing in my ears
My mind sings sweet melodies, but is it a dream?
Soon I will know or at least hopefully

A Lost love

The love that I had once put behind me has resurfaced
The love has resurfaced to the degree of mind changing matters
I've thought about the minor things that hold me back continuously and accepted all of the possibilities that lie ahead of me
My life lies in the hands of a higher power and he determines my destiny
Though I've always wanted this so bad that I could bleed
It has been pushed away only never to be revealed

The love that I had once put behind me has resurfaced
The love has resurfaced to the degree of mind changing matters
And now all that matters is you
You completing me and making me whole
Me reliving the past love that we once shared is the greatest adventure that one could endure
Me releasing all my fears that I have let go and learned to open up and accept who you are and how much you mean to me
I am no longer afraid to accept these feelings for a lost love can only be found once

A doubtful mind has no limitations as to what is misinterpreted
Has no room for positive expansions; has no room for love
A doubtful mind has the negativity of a lost soul not trying to find a home
A doubtful mind has its beliefs and basis it off of actual realness and perception
A doubt mind will not grow unless it is allowed to breathe and believe again
No room for trust leaves no room for love…
And even with love a doubtful mind has no room for a relationship

Some people don't get a 2nd chance

From birth to death we learn to love but by nature we love our parents for who they are good or bad my dad happens to be part of the good. He loves me and my siblings for who we are. Us as individuals, he is forgiving, accepting, and kind of stubborn at being understanding but somehow he always comes around. He has a very busy schedule that doesn't always include his children but all in all he works hard for each one of us. He believes that we will do our best at whatever challenges we take on and for the most part he is willing to help. He's someone I would love to be closer to and have a better relationship with but he's still my dad and I appreciate what I have and the time I can get. Looking back I'm sure I've been more of a problem than some of my other brothers and sisters but I mean no harm to him or myself. I love my dad no matter what he thinks of me or the things that I do and all I ask is that he continues to love me too.

To be fucked up

Being twisted is like being out of your mind
But what is being out of your mind
In reality you are out of yourself and to be out of yourself is to loose your identity
The new you becomes like Dr. Jekyll or Mr. Hyde
A hidden identity
A secret message
Your inner thoughts and spirits escape and you become new…
A new you, a new being
Yet you explore the deep secrets that you allow to stay within
You explore the new feelings that you have under the influence and
You explore the new you …
Who is that…you have no idea but you feel them from within
They speak to you in both spirit and mind
They do you with what is left inside
Until you drift off to sleep warm thoughts flow…and spread across your mind
Your face glows as you
Drift off into another stage of being fucked up

Untitled

When looking for love where do you search?
If you look in either direction there is nothing
Yet your wholeness is not enough
Companionship travels far
As music mellows out my inner soul
Peace sits still yet I desire love, I'm ready and willing to do my best
How do I prove it to someone who doesn't know me?
I ask that you open your eyes to a new experience

I love the person that I was raised to be
I also hate the person that I am at times
I have crossed the two different types of lifestyles that I have grown up to be
Now I'm just screwed up in the head and sensitive to people
I haven't always been quick to realize when I'm getting messed over or not,
Especially when you find it easier to give people the benefit of the doubt (talk about confusion)
But people continue to encourage change
I am who I am and I can't please 'em all
I am honest and helpful
I am loyal and true
Yet someone always finds a way to complain about shyt that I do

I love the person I was raised to be but I also have learned to love the person that I am
Acceptance starts with me…but will never end with you

Distance Afar

The distance between two is hard to deal with
The distance is much longer than the time it seems
To be so far yet so close is unbearable
To not be able to reach out and touch you
When love is just a phone call away
Weeks and weeks go by yet someday is better than none
Alone for the period of time
A period that seems to never end
Just around the corner, up the block, and down the road
Somewhere not too far...
Come closer, bring yourself to me child, and come closer so I can feel...
Feel the distance that keeps us apart come together
I wanna be near you

What is it?

Is it in me or not
What makes me so different?
So undesirable
I mean I have determination
Goals, dreams, and aspirations
But what am I missing?
What don't I have…?

I mean…I guess I realize
What I don't have
Something along the lines of a small mind, a cold heart
no brains, or just plain ole beauty
But is that what it takes
Is that what you desire?

I can't compare or prepare myself enough for you
So what shall I do?
Bow down and cater to the what not's of the world
or stand tall and strong with a broken heart on my own

My loneliness desires a companion
One that's compatible
One who will love and cherish me to the end of time

Who I am

My inner soul represents the true meaning of love
A love that is meaningful and full of color
The color of the rainbows through day and night
The colors that reveal the true meaning of life
The love and harmony that overfills my cup
The peace and serenity that is never enough
The earth and nature that God brings to light
The midst in the morning and dew at night
So, these colors I wear proud because
I am the true meaning of love
And my family takes pride in who we are
    The rainbow

My life is...

My life is a work of art not just beauty alone but a true masterpiece... a masterpiece within itself because of all the shyt I've been through to get here! A masterpiece within for only some to see. The life that I live yet so alone. Alone with disbelief that one day you will come home. Come home to me to hold to hold me oh so tight. Come home to me to make your day and night. To hold, to nurture, to care, so sweet. Only to be there for you even when shyt's too deep because deep down inside no one will be there like me. Yet my life...my life is such a mystery to those on the outside looking in when my only answer is we can just be friends. For my mind is set on what I want and how I live my life. This is untrue to the naked eye. Yet my life is what my life is...because I long to be with you.

The none stressed way:

The non stressed way to life is to rid yourself of anything in your way hindering; mind boggling, etc...Stressed is handled differently by each individual some smoke, drink, fight, yell-you know. My stress has been all of the mentioned above though there was unconditional love. All love ain't good love and all love ain't necessary either. Having the one that I love caught in the midst of my stressful issues and my blue days never seemed to end. She was so sweet and so supportive and one day all that took a 360° on me that shyt faded into the land of the lost. I felt so bad but what was I to do something that I've yearned for all the days of my life don't loose it and don't let it go. My stress all in all was out to get me to drown me into the sea. Had to look at the big picture and make everything so sweet, so peaceful but damn that shyt's hard. It gets better, just don't stop trying ...point blank period if you see stress knocking don't open the door. Love yourself not someone else's problems.

Oh how it hurts

My pain stimulated from within
My mind left thoughtless
The grief felt from the time we departed
The moments of time stood still

I take with me your soul
Your image sitting in the back of my mind
Causes me mental blockage
My thoughts of anything else is non existing

How can I go on?
I hurt because you're not here
I dream just to hear your voice…
to see that beautiful image of the gray haired woman that once existed here on earth

I laughed with you and I cried for you to understand my pain
Yet you listened and laughed not mentioning how you ached how vain
Your body tired and weary, your soul set free
And one day you left this earth peacefully without me

I love you dearly and always will
Because you were MY grandmother and always will be
Like a comforting mother to shield me from harm
Yet you watch me from heaven now with open arms
Awaiting me to join you one day.
Oh how I pray it will be a wonderful reunion

To be with you with laughter and tears
For you to help me overcome my fears…
Fears of being alone on this earth
There's no place like heaven after birth

Cont'd

I love you Grandma Perkins with all my heart
You were my great gram but stepped up to the plate
when my real grandmother one didn't
The one and only who had love for all and told you like it is…

Before you left your eyes glistened, I cried myself to sleep knowing I'd rendered my soul

Emptiness

Disbeliefs become overshadowing
Laying here like a body in a casket
Lifeless yet a peaceful image
Only my mind wanders
Thoughts of movement, timeless moments and that one thing to share
The energy draining slowly into a bucket awaiting disposal
My heart beats as I taste the softness of love
Pound by pound collected without purchase
I deserve more than to lie here alone and without
When I have so much to offer

Overcoming

Is it because I represent my incorrectly or is it because I only understand myself
When do we begin to show that prejudice does not need to exist?
When do we let go of typical myths and stereotypes
How can I overcome my struggle if no one else can…?
When do we start thinking for ourselves?

See everyone has some type of flaw
or better yet some twisted way of thinking
Why is it so important for people to worry about what another person has going on for themselves
Does it effect your life directly?
Or are you looking to make headlines with the next poster board statement

In a common world it would be more beneficial if we could all get along
Set aside our personal views for the sake of accomplishments
Stop tearing others down for their beliefs
Stop tearing others down for who they are
but instead build them up and make them grand

Awareness

My soul aches, my eyes burn red, I bleed disparity upon my dreary days
I look at myself as a life that has been dead-ended
Awaiting the day that light will shimmer across the dry sand that burdened my heart
The glorification for being able to love
To feel something deep on the inside and being uplifted on the outer surface
My body shivers upon the air blowing past the hardness of the skin
But is this a shell
A shell that is unpryable or is it one that waits to be cracked opened and explored from within
Oh how do I let you uncover my inner feelings
How do I explain my emotions when my soul aches and my eyes burn red me bleeding disparity on my dreary days
I want to be loved but am I capable of accepting it?
Is this my biggest problem? How can I fear the awaiting?
How shall I be discovered?
When shall I be revealed?

New Orleans, LA 2005

Abandoned street corners and homes in slum villages below sea level. Here floods can ruin lives but here live smiling faces and eager spirits. Alligators and crawfish in the swamps; bayous that provide basic nutrients to all. The waters are some peoples main money source yet their biggest enemy as well. If AIDS don't kill them first what will? Pickpocketers and scam artist have their hustle but if you know that everyone's resources are limited, why take from the people who are poor with nothing left but their Hope and their love for God. Most survive with what they have but for those who have given up, they roam the streets for their next trick or treat only to gain a dollar for a blow or hit, but tell me who looks out for them? Well here they are considered trash in the streets. Walk past and glance but don't give or speak, just see the un-existing image that is in the image of a man. The same man that was given life by the man up above. If he accepted and forgave then why can't we? Survival of the fittest or every man for themselves, how selfish is that? These folks here whether rich or poor feel any superiority than the next when they are all at risk. One day whether natural death, disease, or disaster they will all be free. Maybe God will keep his eye on them and treat them just as he holds Project Lazarus*. Miracles happen where beliefs are high and dreams soar. So my question is why can't we all turn nothing into something together?

Project Lazarus is a hospice/nursing home for Men who have been infected by HIV/AIDS some have no family and die alone, others have visitors until their times come. I participated in a volunteering experience with my University at the time.

Hidden Secrets

Something deadly and very much diseased
Unpleasantly painful and utterly tiring
The death defying virus that becomes full blown
It entraps the soul from the inside out
Distorting minds and disabling bodies
Causing a chain reaction of downhill events for some
and an uphill climb for strength for others
This virus is H.I.V. and it's the #1 killer
of a lot of heterosexual men and women
But why????
Is it the I.V. drug use or the sex that makes them think
They are invincible…but shit happens
Let go of the pride y'all and get tested
Cause the next pretty young thang that will be laying next to you or shot into your arm….. will be 22 bottles of empty medications, three bouquets of flowers
representing the three letters you could have avoided H.I.V. because he never implied his versatility……

Creation

Do you like the juices that flow from the streams and valleys below to a bitter creek?
Do you like the sweet taste that awaits…?
From my inner peace connected to your sweet and subtle soul
You loose yourself into my river and we become as one; one taste, one small piece of that condemned mind abandoned and left behind
To reconnect with what is real
To remember how it feels
To have that river always flowing into…
…into a pool of love where my inner peace connected to your soul

Sometimes new beginnings aren't as easy as they should be
Qualities under estimated by quantities
Multitude of energy to enhance so much but you'd rather pass
Selfishness on both parts but it's my time to shine too
Soak it up while you can

Letting Go

To loose you once is more than enough
But to loose you forever it's harder to do
My completeness, my happiness is non the less finished

You made each moment worth while
Our love plentiful, our souls relaxed
Together united as one, our bond solid as a rock
Our souls glowed brighter than the moon

You're given the option of letting me go
Yet you choose to stay close underneath my wing
You cling to me and my soul
So tightly almost forgetting to breathe

Relax my love
I'm gone not dead
Instead of weeping with blistering red eyes
Rejoice for you have learned one more life lesson and that is…
Just because you've lost the person doesn't mean you have to loose the feelings

Untitled

Surrounded by a world where every man is for themselves, a world of young mothers without goals, a broken soul, and a no good baby daddy scarred by the STD's and bruises received to the eye. The heart with no training and damn sho no start. No starting knowledge of how to prevent the un-expectable and no strength to reject those that mean us no good. We search for that which is good only to find that we become stuck between a rock and a hard place. Awaiting the shift of the world instead of maneuvering our way out of our tight binds…We let go of our broken hearts and desolate souls and become the respectable young women that we are. You should want more out of life.

A Place within

A place within me is my surrounding energy
It is not defeatable but has high potential for determination

A place within me is a small cubby hole that has been left empty at this time
But it is definitely refillable

A place within me lies a young woman that has dignity, self-esteem, and is lead by her spirituality and her self-righteous beliefs

A place within myself is for me
It is not to be tormented by any other
It is to be cherished and genuinely stroked

This place within me is in my heart

My social status is what you think of me
due to attribution you have prejudged me
But look beyond what you see young men
and go beyond what you hear ladies
My social status is just that...
A place in the world that has pointed me out on a scale of many
To say who they think I am but my support lies within self
What I have is unimportant so why defend my social status
For in this world I will only be identified by a number......

Now ask yourself are you really important as you think you are?????

When a warm soul turns cold

My soul that was once filled with warmth has now gone cold
My soul that was once filled with energy has now been torn
Worn and weary, scarred and unrepaired my warm soul has now gone cold
I lost my warmth because of you
I lost my energy because I was blue
My soul cried out for you and you didn't answer
My tears made a path for you and you didn't follow
My heart melted and you didn't mold it

My warm soul that was once filled with warmth and energy has now turned cold
In response to you, I lift my head to free myself of all that was dead
Dead because I opened my door and you didn't come in
Dead because I loved you so much and not myself in the end
But now I see that I must love me and let you go…
Go on to a new someone or thing
Because now you see all good things come to an end

My warm soul that had gone cold is now burning and is overflowed
Overflowed with life, love, and peace of mind
This warmth of mine I can't leave behind

It's important to me to keep it burning and remain humble with my warm soul glowing
Never again will I in the end, let my warm soul turn cold
I am my own friend

My revelation

From beginning of time my plan was defined
By a man, no other than the great one himself
To live and learn the intricate details that life would have to offer
The mishaps and unfortunate road blocks
Manage people in and out of my life
An unexpected childhood that only made life seem as a mere dream
But it wasn't reality no one said you can't have any and everything you want
It really wasn't meant to be as perfect as his plan
My survival was to be determined by my strength
Although sometimes weak I managed to survive the worst
An unbelievable childhood and young adult life
If only I knew what adulthood would have to offer?
My revelation incomplete
My revelation will determine me
For the man above sees all and means well
Let's hope the ending of my life will be much greater than the beginning

<u>For my soror</u>

Faulty failures, fears, frowns, and foes
What a difficult road I've managed to confront
Confusion blurs my thoughts and love rules my heart
Are my concerns and doubts reasonable?
Is there a reason behind my actions?
For I am holding on to this mere image of excellence and joy
yet I feel heartache and pain
This road needs to be crossed but which foot will proceed or
will I ever forever have the fear of progressing?
See I realize that I am living a ...mmmmhhhhh....
Well now honestly let me rethink that...
See I realize that I am merely selling myself a dream
A dream that is a realm of unrealistic desires and unpleasant future
But only I hold the key to my future and now I know that I must proceed...
head and feet first across this difficult road
        For I am not afraid

Discovering/Reconfiguring Me

Sometimes it's hard to determine my wants. My mind plays many indecisive games with me. I can't determine what's real or fake anymore. It's hard for me to sleep and I have no clear understanding of much of anything dealing with myself. I questioned a lot of my life issues and choices I made met my parent's expectation in comparison to mine. Do I love differently or do I even want to be loved at all. Why can't I accept the no's and yes's that are right in my face? How can I avoid some situations? It has been said that I speak before thinking and maybe I'm not as "large" as I appear to be…I can accept that but I never feel or attempt to be larger than others. For I am just as unworthy as they may be or may not be. Many times I just want to shut down and not voice my opinion to others because I don't want to appear like a know it all. Negativity surrounds my mind because I know no other way to view a positive statement that is misunderstood. I want to care, to be different, to not be like my parents in some ways but I don't know how not to. From today on I will not be so difficult, so complex, and argumentative when misunderstood, unsure, and keep my extreme "negative" thoughts to myself. I will continue to be real but speak less you know… have some tact. I would rather not be seen or heard at this point. I will avoid anything that shows my "greatness" as a person. I am reconsidering self. I am reconsidering life. Is it what I'm supposed to love or am I suppose to just survive it. I am reconsidering me…I am smaller than I appear. My internal struggle is greater than any given day or struggle that exist right now.

You existed

A chance of a lifetime to grow with you
How can one ever let that pass
I look to hold you at night but no one is there
Your smile brighter than the moon's glow
The joy you bring with love that overflows
A scent sweeter than a rose at night
A garden that gives us air to breathe right
With skies that deliver the world's light
Caress me with your touch
Open my ears to your voice
Oh how I miss thee even when you're here
You are a song bird in another life waiting to hear my voice
Because you are my all, my everything, you're a part of my life
I gave to thee all I had and yet I had nothing to give
I took in your load just as you had done
And with that we embraced a moment of a lifetime…
                To be continued

Starting over

As the hour passes there is a full moon
As the seasons change we loose room…
Room for those who weren't on shit from the beginning of time
I have left behind those days where things and feelings go unanswered
Those days when hopes become disasters
My peace unlocks my soul, my heart is melted gold
My tears drop and drain like a down pour of rain
Into the street corners gutter drains
For I can not do it, I will not do it
For there's a full moon and I have accepted
Accepted a new beginning

???able Emotions

Why when I wake up do I not look forward to interacting with people?
What is it that draws me away?
Why is it that some people rub me the wrong way?
I can't allow them to get under my skin but
I can not control the frustration I feel
How do I know what is real? I want to be friendlier
I want to be more kind
I think I can't do it because I'm so behind
Behind from where I should be in my lifetime with my emotions
Is this my punishment or is it a lie?
How do I let them go?
How do I rid them of my life?
Should I seek professional help?
Or do I need advise?

Emotions are really hard to understand when you are uncertain of what exactly you are feeling. But exploration is the key to becoming a better YOU. You may have many ups and downs through the process but stick with it in time they will be revealed and understandable.

Real love

When love comes it's the first knock at the door
Things begin to happen simultaneously
The quiver in your stomach and the pounding in your chest
Your palms sweat
Your body temperature reaches its peak

When loves come you start doing things you never imagined
You begin laughing and smiling at the sight of nothing
You enjoy the slightest bit of interest unexpectedly

When love comes your eyes glisten
Your face glows
Joy is in the air
Music sounds more beautiful than before

When love comes the experience is unimaginable
The memory engraved
The purpose fulfilled
Just as air represents its name
When love comes its breathless and
It carries you to a mental fortress afar

Social Norms

Is it okay for her to be called a bitch if she acts like a hoe
Shall we call him a fag because he is a virgin at 24?
Why must I be labeled a dyke because I have short hair?
These social stereotypes "depict" social norms but social norms are not all legit
It is what most people do but most people are not you, so who begins to break these rules
These social stereotypes that seem to rule; rule the earth for men and women
Tearing the bonds of friends and foes
If my view of the world is hate, shall I be antisocial and not participate in the change that needs to come about because this world singles out all humans as a whole
And why that happens no one will ever know
Just remember most of us were born alone and no one has to fit into the social norms

So again I say

Is it okay for her to be called a bitch if she acts like a hoe and
Shall we call him a fag because he is still a virgin at 24?
No we should let them be whoever they want
For it is those qualities that give them their own personality
Those qualities that begin to break the social norms
We must begin to rid and reduce the social stereotypes before they are applied to one of our own....

How would you feel if you had a stigma applied to you?

Who I take home

When I sleep at night enveloped in the moon light with sweat dripping from my brow
The daily interaction of our love flowing and smiles as bright as the sun
Who I take home is my own damn business
When I step out of my box and I do my thang at the end of the night
Who I take home is my own damn business
So now that I'm grown and feelings of being alone
Alone forever because…because of my choice between man or woman and my fight between mom and man
My feelings cannot be changed…they will not be changed
Partially because I am grown now momma and it's my choice
So to you I say who I take home is my own damn business
I'm happy, I'm free fuck all of you who judge me
God above is my provider and protector
I fear no human being
I walk with my head high; hand in hand with that woman or man because
Who I take home is my own damn business
I love that woman like I would love that man and
I'll continue to be free and take her home time after time
For no one is going to steal my joys about life or whip my behind because
Who I take home is my own damn business

S/N: I'm just venting because I need people to support me or mind their own business. I can never do anything right in the eyes of some but I can not live for anyone else other than myself.

I get asked

Sometimes I get asked if I'm a boy or a girl
Sometimes I get stares of confusion but to the confused...
I'm me
Seemingly part man mentally and part woman physically
I know some of you may find it hard to understand....
But see I admire the strengths of a man both sexually and mentally
But I adore the power of a woman, the sexiness of her style
I appreciate them both, if I had a choice I would be <u>me</u> because I would be able to explore both sides of my destiny just as I do
I didn't ask to feel this way but I feel that I live as a combination of man and woman inside out but
Don't get it twisted 70% man sexually and mentally and 30% woman
True I bleed, look, and sometimes act as a woman may do but then again with each reflection that exist aside of me being me I use to ask myself
Where did I go wrong???
There is no wrong for men and women role play all the time so consider me playing my role literally "all the time"
I love my role for I am content; I'm proud, happy and comfortable most importantly
I will be able to provide...provide for my future just as a man would do... and some even believe as a man should do only I'll still have the power of a woman
I shall always remain 70% man, 30% woman but 100% ME
Believe that and live with it

S/N: I remember being a little girl maybe around nine and my dads sister told me you should have been a boy....you sit wrong, dress wrong, you just too rough and girls don't act like you do. I told her maybe I should have been a boy but unfortunately I'm not. I have always been tomboyish my entire life. I am not comfortable in girl clothes, I don't wear makeup, I've never being prissy, and putting forth my best attempt to look fabulous is far from my concern. I love my plainness, my jeans, my sweat shirts, and my gym shoes and I always will.

I looked for you

I looked for you, yet you were nowhere to be found
I searched for you, yet I couldn't find that lead to you
With open arms spread wide and love to share
I opened my heart to your mind
Yet you wrapped it around your finger and twirled it round so tight

I looked for you, yet I feel like you hid
I searched for you, yet I couldn't find you
Where did you go? You were just here
Wanting me and looking to keep me close
You said you loved me and wanted me by your side to the very end
To be your lover and your friend

I looked for you, yet I couldn't find you
I searched for you, yet you were no where to be found
I opened my heart to your heart and
you responded but only for a short time
You turned away so many times only to return once more
and then leave me behind
But again I looked for you…
And you were there waiting to embrace the joy that I bring

I still love you

Speechless

Excited to see you to hear your voice
To dream of the scent of your body
Your quiver from your touch
You turn me on in every way
You mentality floats above the stars
The clouds and the moon so clear
I hold you close and feel you breathe
You moan to my touch and cling to me
Your eyes so brown
Your lips shine for me
I bite my lip and breathe slow
Thinking of how I want you more
To caress my every curve and bless the fluids below
You yearn for it and I give it to you upon asking
You receive me completely and then it's off to sleep
To marinate in the love making session that we just shared
Oh how I wish it would last
But in time it'll come again
And you await that moment

His Fight

Undisclosed energy guarded by a steel heart
Wanting companionship but doesn't want to start
to feel whatever may hurt his soul from inside out
Wounded scars slowly covered by comfort
He rejects it time after time
Desiring the intimacy with no connection
He fails, feelings creep inward and yet he continues to push
Denying himself of something soothing to the heart
He sulks in the moisture conditioning his skin and mind
Melting to the warm wonders inside
He fails, yet he continues to guard his heart
Desiring the intimacy with no connection
The only guarantee is that we will grow apart

Blood Flowing

My body bleeds for love; can you feel it with touch
My heart releases its aches; my soul has been pierced
My stomach turns; I hear my heart beat
My blood is flowing in and out of every part of my body
Like a freshwater river providing to all
It is not pure; it is not clean because it has been tainted
Tainted with pain and un-pleasurable desires
Uncontrollable emotions that feels so right
I look to feel your heart beat with mine
I look to have our juices intertwined
My body bleeds for love; can you feel it with touch
Warm on the inside but not on the out
My blood is flowing and my heart bleeds
Come closer to me now or never
Come feel it too; share this moment I have for you
Hold me tight so that it overflows
Into a puddle of love and you have control
For just a moment I give you my all
To feel my blood flowing into your heart
Accept it, hold it, mold it, and love it
For I have given a piece of me to you…
…a piece that yearns for you
Those uncontrollable emotions that feels so right
My body bleeds for your love each and every night

In time I will find if it is true
In time I will see you my dream come true
Deep within me is something growing like a rose waiting to bloom
My inner soul has spoken and my body has responded
How do I accept the answers as truth?
How do I begin to understand the change?
I speak to God and he tells me grow my child for it is beneficial for you
There you shall be in the end a brand new person
With a fresh mind and a clean soul
I grow with you because it is time to learn more and see new things
Sometimes change can be a good thing

Like a rose waiting to bloom in time I will find if it is true
In time I will see you my dream come true
In time I will be able to determine if I can love again
Love a person for who they are
Love despite of this broken heart
My dream that aches and blurs my mind
A dream that I feel is so far behind
Behind me for it is love that stinks so bad that I can feel it deep within my stomach
Tossing and turning yet not burning to feel the sensation that offers happiness

In time I will find if it is true
In time I will see you my dream come true
In time that growing deep within will be out and that rose will bloom and die
I will be able to determine if I can love again

How could you do it?

When did you loose it? Where did it go?
You let loose and did not show
You gave into the world of darkness that's evil and death
How could you do it?
Why didn't you care?
Let go of your feelings
Let go of yourself
Your life, your spirit, your sons last breathe
When did you loose it?
Where did it go?
How come no hope? Why did you go?
Down the same road that caught you once
That road that goes into your vein,
the dark long road that stole your life
mmph and now you want it back…
back to do the same shyt all over again
You gave into the world of darkness
…of evil and pain
You did not show it but when you did loose it
Where did it go? How could you do it?
Same old excuses…
but let me guess it wasn't you

S/N: a struggling addict without real support is only a setup for relapse but even when you give all you can, to keep that person positive, if they wanna go back then they do just that!!
Don't become an enabling co-dependent regardless of the situation……you only keep them sicker!!!

Baton Rouge, LA (*purpose and date unknown*)

There is a separation that exist between us I seen it clear in my dream
Though I never seen it face to face my dream was vivid it was alive
How can we be so silly? How can we be so blind?
Who the fuck thought they were God
Back in my ancestor's time why was there segregation
For shit like food and water
Why was there segregation for where you would defecate?
Didn't they know we were equal and as strong as them?
Didn't they think that it wouldn't last forever?
How could they not care?
In the eyes of man some women were set below...
But how could it be admissible that an entire culture and race was No Good
Didn't they know we were equal and as strong as them?
How could one man be so silly yet alone in an entire crowd?
How could they all be blind?
Who the fuck made them God
Despite their devilish ways
Well I'll tell those racist asshole one thing
My God is an awesome God if you know what I mean
He took away all the segregation for generations to come...

Casual Affair

Holding on to you as if there is no end
Awakened by the sunrise
Glistening images that provide strength
But pillars of pain standing tall
Built from the many inconsistencies that come with life
Internally aching from pain and desiring genuine love
A casual affair only inflicts more long term pain
I'm afraid…
Afraid you'll hurt me yet you deny that as your intention
Love is meant to be amazingly unconditional with good and bad; highs and lows
But how do I trust that when I have pillars of pain
and the normality's of my life has been short lived
I desire to be held and touched in the ways that please you

In a casual affair that only inflicts more long term pain
I'm afraid…
Afraid to be hurt again
Not in a hurry but uncertainties soaring
Unsure of the flow of direction
Will my path ever be clear?
Knowing that darkness and clouds leave
only for sunlight to come back in…
But pillars of pain standing tall
Awaiting the wrecking balls destruction date
Until then this casual affair can only go so far

Recognizing me

I noticed you, yet you failed to acknowledge my presence
An opportunity to grow and option to pass
A missed hit where quality means much less than quantity
This woman of substance breaks down slowly
Tears fall saddened by the thought of dismissing the days to come
Each abandoned one turning into rain drops
Rain drops that drench this woman of substance
Submerging her into a fallen guilt of displeasure…
Displeasure to the thought of how many men pass up good things
I guess that saying some men leave their mark and some a stain
can attest for how many real men still exist?
As I noticed you, yet you failed to acknowledge me
My last tear dropped…
My last tear drop didn't turn into rain
It didn't turn into rain because my last tear drop left a stain
a stain to remind me that I AM…
a woman of substance

It happened

He lifted me
He lifted me higher than any substance could ever supply
I mean he got me open…
Open like the effects of Vick's vapors up your nose
He lifted me

The connection so intense and awaiting its time
That built up pleasure that was left behind
Behind never to explore like a forbidden secret
but the door opened and I let you in
To experience the moment that we've waited for years to share
He lifted me

I mean he got me open
Considering things that I laid to rest
Nawl it ain't his dick or the size of his chest
But skin so brown and lips so round
Personality complimentary and full of life
How could I be resistant to such a sight?
He lifted me

He lifted me
He lifted me higher than any substance could ever supply
He allowed me to feel again…
Things that I've lacked for years
He lifted me in all the right places
and then we released the experience that was awaited for

A shared moment to be remembered
Now it's ended

<u>Confusion</u>

Caught between heart and mind
Tossing around thoughts of reality and unrealistic wants
Knowing the difference between my desires and expectations
Completeness just around the corner lurking on a slow prowl
Afraid to meet…Afraid to connect
Confusion keeps you far away with mixed feelings to hide
Yet confusion pushes me further because I have no time
Time to taunt and toil with my heart
One beat away from destiny
Embarrassing wholeness as underlying feelings resurface
Do you exist with meaning or is there no purpose?
Similarities soaring high we share that common bond in many ways
Speculations show you desire more but only time will tell
Imagery of love making
Enwrapped in the warmth presented
Caressing of the soul…We share each other
Yet we're caught between heart and mind
Tossing around thoughts of reality and unrealistic wants
Knowing the difference between our desires and expectations
Completeness around the corner lurking on a slow prowl…
Will we meet or will we continue to walk on opposite sides of the streets
I wanna know

Masturbation

I pictured you stroking me
Every inch of my satin silk skin
You caress my nipples and tickle my navel
with your tongue down to my unforeseen treasures

I pictured you stroking me
Mentally in all the right ways
The desirable intimacy in High Definition form
You run across every synaptic nerve in my brain
I process you…as…I…I

I pictured you stroking me inside out
My warm wonders explode and melt for you
But you are only a figment of my imagination
For the time being…

I pictured you stroking me
So stiff and slow
My inhale gets deeper as my erection grows
Blood pumping and clit rising…
I pictured you stroking me as I touched myself
I pictured you stroking me to the pulsation of my cum

R U Serious?

Irrational thoughts lay deep within the misconception of our friendship
Envy of materialistic things
Wants of placing yourself above your current status
Are you growing on me? Or moving to quickly?
I say slow down yet you profess your desires to become more than friends
Conversation unsatisfying to my taste buds...
Please remind me how old are you again?
Look my child pump your breaks before you find yourself
Sulking in an unpleasant unwanted experience of a distorted fantasy
That previewed differently in your mind
Listen to the unmentioned conversation by watching my demeanor
Cringe at the sign of confrontation
I won't feed into your fountain of youth
For your satisfaction
Instead I rather imagine the day reality sets within
So please understand that the movie you previewed that mapped out the unrealistic views of life, love, and relationships
failed for having poor quality and failure to present a good plot

I breathe in and exhale a mouthful of nothing
My pen in my hand with nothing but writers block
My mind preoccupied with a beautiful image of pure chocolate bliss
Mind racing thoughts through a cloud so thick
Can you clear the fog?
The sound of music soft and relaxing
Yet that beautiful image stands strong
I'm seeing you perfect whole and complete
I'm seeing you…my beautiful image before I drift off to sleep

I've been told that giving up is not hard to do....
I believe this to be true
It's staying on track that keeps me rattled
My dreams to do something big
And my abilities to grow
Yet my interferences make me wonder
Exactly how far I will go?
My anxiety always high because of my past and
My present... wondering
If I try what will be my outcome
See I had gotten so use to being a let down to others
That I became unsure of which way to go
Confirmation to my struggles were tagged and labeled
Dyslexia...a hindrance to my comprehension and ability to express my thoughts clearly
Frustrated that I have to go over things multiple times
I usually feel like I have fallen behind
Wanting to give up because my focus unsteady
Yet my determination is imperative because I am ready
Ready to succeed in all that I have planned
Ready to settle down and have all I can
Properly medicated all has calmed down
At least for now
I can now tackle some of my dreams

Dangerous Signs

Red flags appear and disappear as I continue to get to know you
Inconsistencies in your character and goals for yourself
Uninterested in the company you want to keep with me
but solemnly in the stimulation you present to my mind
My desires feel unmet and unchallenged
Whole yet incomplete
Your interest lies within yourself and then I come along
Never secondary to any human being
I am wonderful in my own way
I am my perfect human being
I feel like I'm floating on an almost punctured raft
Waiting for the day I will sink and disappear
Into the darkness that I feel when you think of me
I'm back to the basics with life …and it doesn't include you!!!

Temptation

As we lay side by side
the urge to move upon you as quickly as a predator awaiting his prey crosses my mind
The smoothness of your skin as soft as a baby's bottom
Your scent ever so pleasant and tempting

In my dreams it was all that I imagined
The initial contact
all the way down to the intimate embrace
The taste of pure honey melts in my mind
Lasting effects and impressions still linger

Unchallenged in my pursuit
I attack only to be received with enjoyment of each and every touch
The sounds escalate slowly following each moan of excitement
The passion flowing freely with intensity

The temptation irresistible and the passion unexplainable...

Loneliness

To be without
Feelings of incompleteness
Many days without a special figure
to hold and love in your life
Weeks and days dragging on
An empty bed
A small hole in your heart
Loneliness is every day that no one knows you count
The feeling you get when one has the inability to see that you're special
Every holiday without family and loved ones
It's when time allows you to feel each hour, min, and second
Loneliness is what I feel…
Alone is how I spend most of my days

<u>Open your eyes</u>

Just as invisible as I have always imagined myself
A blurred image with a microscopic view
A picture painted on the perfect canvas yet it's impossible to see
A memory pasted of what could have been your present life
What went wrong?
What was not seen?
The immediacy and concern that was available to you
The impossibility of ever having something so close to perfection
The communication that went unheard, the lack of…
The lack of energy put into everything else but it…Why?
How could you forget what's good to you?
What's good for you?
How could you be so blinded to miss this beautiful image waiting to be explored?
Held and cared for with the upmost respect
Sheltered and nurtured like it was my last breath
The picture once painted on the perfect canvas is fading…
and only the memory will last

Finding me

With each breathe I desire to let go
Let go all the pain and hurt that lies within
The freedom to move around without a past that continue to haunt me
The life that allows openness to be one's self

With each breath I remain hopeful of a new day
A new day for a new beginning
A new me, to share and be at peace with myself
To love more from within
To re-create my destiny that sometime appears empty

To become whole… to feel every emotion for what it is worth
To understand the reasons behind the happenings to live again
To smile more freely and engage myself willingly

To have a fair chance at a sweet life

My Reality

My reality wants to be filled with joy
It seeks honesty and appreciation
My reality desires to be cared for with
an equality that exist between two

My reality is hard earned yet freely flowing once obtained
My reality is what I have made of it
A joy like no other
The additional reason to smile each morning
The peacefulness that remains ever flowing from within

My reality is not selfish, nor self-centered
It does not boast nor leaves one to be forgotten
It is a pure energy of love and fairness
It is................................

My reality and only special people are drawn to it

Moving Backward

As I turned and took one last look I as was leaving…
Leaving my peace
Leaving a space I built for two years now only to turn back
I'm going "Home"
Finally thought I was out for good "Damn Economy"
Never thought I'd turn back (looking forward)
Uneasy every night that I lay my head tossing and turning
Is this so called "Home" really meant for me anymore?
Or am I just exaggerating the intensity of my desires
to not exist here anymore
Well when no "family" is at home
I wonder will I get to truly be me
Therefore wondering how can I call it "Home"?

Unspoken Thoughts

At a continuous loss of words what does this mean?
Nothing new or are things better?
Where did the unspoken language of words go?
Disappeared right before my eyes
A possibility to let it all out and time just ticks away
Seems like those mere words that related to life
faded all so quickly
How do I connect now?
What is the right thing to say?
What will this pen produce just yet?

Summer Breeze

Completed with a whisk of crisp air across your face
The smell of freshness at the morning dew
The sun reflecting God's image through its rays
The sounds of people from all places
The smells of garbage overflowing
The blue-green water image of the ocean spreads wide
The calmness of the dark with clear night skies
The stars beaming down twinkles of love
The energy that connects us feels so warm
The summer breeze gives us Hope…
The summer breeze leaves a lasting impression

Stunted

Challenged by another's ignorance
Attempts to keep the connection open
That thing we keep working on discreetly
The bond that brings us all together
Our uniqueness varies but still we share a commonality
Not certain where the arrogance and ego's superiority surfaces from
But we arose from the cloth that was bound by three letters BΦΩ
So what do those letters mean?
Can we take it back to where and what it was suppose to be?
Can we start all over again as one, perfect, whole and complete?
Can we reconnect our purpose and drive it on home?
Let's get back to the beginning and let loose the egos

Turmoil

With times changing and kids dying because of everyday turmoil
What do you to look forward too?
A potential future…

A future where you desire your loved ones to be supportive
To be present in a moment that could be life changing and an everlasting memory

A memory that you can never get back more than once
A memory that could be the key to a better life
A life dreamed of with the right support
A life desired…

A life that is at a stand still
Because I desire my mother to be involved yet
She doesn't get how her purpose or involvement matters
but she also can't begin to see how it interferes all at the same time

Today was a day that I smiled. I was calm and most importantly I felt free. Free as a bird without any burdens or troubles. My completeness lies within. No priorities or commitments to attend to. Just self-care which is something that has been neglected for many years. Now I spread my wings and soar with open arms above all that life has in store for me. I am free...free to be me and free to do it as planned.....but carefully.

Grateful

It is by Him who allows me to sit with the pen in my hand and I thank Him for giving me life. The testimony to present because for you who don't have a clue. I haven't always loved and accepted myself as imperfect because I was to do no wrong. My life was a blessing that was to carry me far…far until I reached the reality of pain and misery that allowed me to accept me for me. For I alone could not change what He hath laid out for me. I am human, I have feelings, and emotional bouts just like any other except I lack the skills to show them most times, to express my every moment of my hurt. Love and pain that is what I've experienced. It wasn't until failed attempt after failed attempts that I learned to appreciate life and all that it could offer. I am who I am and that is all I can accept of me; for my layout is undetermined and my mind has been set free. Free into his hand for he has a better plan and knowing of my destiny. My God unmovable and none repairable He holds the key, he prepares me for experience after experience and my destiny. Greatness is his gift, life is his option, being able to enjoy either of them is up to me and although I can't change the hand I was dealt I can change how it affects me

About the author

I was born Kenyata Fletcher to Yvonne Finley and Alexander Fletcher in Chicago, IL. I resided on the west side of Chicago for most of my life. I attended Lane Technical High School and continued my college education eventually graduating from Chicago State University (undergrad) and Concordia University (grad). I currently hold a Mater's degree in Community Counseling and I am planning to obtain a Ph. D in Human Services. My passion for helping others has been a part of my make up since an early age. Although, an only child I was taught to give to others without expectation of something in return. My parents were workaholics but instilled great work ethics, respect, and the importance of having an education in me. Even today I carry these values with me because I believe they yield a very important message that many young people seem to lack these days. My plans in writing, living, and giving is to continue serving my community and helping others.

If I can do anything to continue changing the world I would give free education and job training to all Americans so that we all have a better chance to succeed. The standard that I have lived by is to do right by others regardless of how they treat me and I will be rewarded much more than I can see.

You may contact me at kenyatafletcher@yahoo.com with questions, comments, and concerns.

Thank You's

Thank You God for giving me the ability to formulate my feelings into words and always keeping me even when I wanted to give up on everything

My thanks you's go to all of those that have supported me in my dreams, comforted me in my tears, and desired to soar with me each step of the way. Thank you.

To my lil brother DJ and my sister Alexis remember that your voice can always be heard because I'm just a phone call away if you ever need me. I got your backs! I love you two.

To my special friend our trials and tribulations got us far. Your support, encouragement, and love can never be changed in my heart. Thank you for the experience….I will always love you and yours.

To my sisty Marie, I love you from the bottom of my heart. We will never be without each others support.

To my BFF's Kesha, Marilen, Medge….my aces, man I can go on and on about our times. Thank you all for getting me through each hurdle in this book. Yall experienced the most with me and I LOVE YOU ALL forever for that……Ride or die for life!!!!! Dekoven thanks for not turning your back on me when others did…we got each other!!!

To my life long friends Tanika and Niaomi…sometimes I wonder where I would be without you two…boy I can only imagine. I love you both and wish you both the best in life's journey.

To the remainder of my true friends/family please note although I can't name you all there is nothing that I wouldn't do for you. *(Smooches)*

www.ingramcontent.com/pod-product-compliance
Lightning Source LLC
LaVergne TN
LVHW011417080426
835512LV00005B/112